THE CATHOLIC CHURCH AND HOMOSEXUALITY

"If any one lie with a man as with a woman, both have committed an abomination, let them be put to death: their blood be upon them."
—Leviticus 20:13

Desclée, Lefebvre e Cia, Roma & Tournay, 1887

St. Peter Damian (1007-1072)
Bishop, Confessor and Doctor of the Church

St. Peter Damian assisted the 11th-century Popes with moral reform, which included work toward eradicating the vice of homosexuality.

THE CATHOLIC CHURCH AND HOMOSEXUALITY

The Appendix to
IN THE MURKY WATERS OF VATICAN II,
Which is Volume 1 of the Collection
Eli, Eli, Lamma Sabacthani?

By
Atila Sinke Guimarães

"Do not err: neither fornicators, nor idolaters, nor adulterers, nor the effeminate, nor liers with mankind [sodomites] . . . shall possess the kingdom of God."
—1 Corinthians 6:9-10

TAN BOOKS AND PUBLISHERS, INC.
Rockford, Illinois 61105

First published by MAETA, Metairie, Louisiana, as the Appendix to *In the Murky Waters of Vatican II*, 1997. Republished with slight revisions as a separate book by TAN Books and Publishers, Inc. in 1999.

ISBN 0-89555-651-0

Library of Congress Catalog Card No.: 99-70787

Printed and bound in the United States of America.

TAN BOOKS AND PUBLISHERS, INC.
P.O. Box 424
Rockford, Illinois 61105
1999

SACRED SCRIPTURE SAYS . . .

"Thou shalt not lie with mankind as with womankind, because it is an abomination. . . . Defile not yourselves with any of these things with which all the nations have been defiled, which I will cast out before you, and with which the land is defiled: the abominations of which I will visit, that it may vomit out its inhabitants. . . . Beware then, lest in like manner, it vomit you also out, if you do the like things, as it vomited out the nation that was before you. Every soul that shall commit any of these abominations, shall perish from the midst of his people. . . . I am the Lord your God."

—*Leviticus* 18:22-30

"And the Lord rained upon Sodom and Gomorrha brimstone and fire from the Lord out of heaven. And he destroyed these cities, and all the country about, all the inhabitants of the cities, and all things that spring from the earth." —*Genesis* 19:24-25

"For this cause God delivered them up to shameful affections. For their women have changed the natural use into that use which is against nature. And, in like manner, the men also, leaving the natural use of the women, have burned in their lusts one towards another, men with men working that which is filthy, and receiving in themselves the recompense which was due to their error. . . . Who, having known the justice of God, did not understand that they who do such things, are worthy of death; and not only they that do them, but they also that consent to them that do them."—*Romans* 1:26-27, 32

"For if God . . . reducing the cities of the Sodomites, and of the Gomorrhites, into ashes, condemned them to be overthrown, making them an example to those that should after act wickedly. . . . The Lord knoweth how to deliver the godly from temptation, but to reserve the unjust unto the day of judgment to be tormented."

—*2 Peter* 2:4-9

"Be not deceived, God is not mocked." —*Galatians* 6:7

CONTENTS

THE CATHOLIC CHURCH AND HOMOSEXUALITY

"A woman shall not be clothed with man's apparel, neither shall a man use woman's apparel: for he that doeth these things is abominable before God."

—Deuteronomy 22:5

AUTHOR'S NOTE

We remind the Reader that this study was made with regard to the crisis in the clergy and in the religious orders (Chap. X.6), which has to be seen as one of the consequences of conciliar *aggiornamento*. Here we make a detailed analysis of just one of the characteristics of this crisis. We believe that, if necessary, other topics addressed in Item 6 of Chapter X of *In the Murky Waters of Vatican II* could be developed in similar fashion.

AN OVERVIEW

§ 1 In view of the scandals that have taken place in the Church recently, it seems opportune to present an overall view of homosexuality in the post-conciliar crisis in the Church.[1]

The criteria adopted were the following: preferably to leave aside particular cases and to deal with those that reflect general situations; to give priority to news not published in our local press; and to make a summary of the locally published news so that the main points will be remembered.

1. THE POSITION OF CATHOLIC TRADITION REGARDING HOMOSEXUALITY

Excerpts from *Sacred Scripture*

§ 2 In the ***Old Testament*** Scripture refers to the vice of homosexuality with special severity:

- "And the Lord said: The cry of Sodom and Gomorrha is multiplied, and their sin is become exceedingly grievous" (*Gen.* 18:20).
- The angels arrived at Lot's house, under the appearance of two handsome men. "But before they went to bed, the men of the city beset the house both young and old, all the people together. And they called Lot, and said to him: Where are the men that came in to thee at night? Bring them out hither that we may know them. . . . And they pressed very violently upon Lot; and they were even at the point of breaking open the doors. And behold the men [angels] put out their hand, and drew in Lot unto them, and shut the door. And them that were without, they struck with blindness from the least to the greatest, so that they could not find the door" (*Gen.* 19:4-11).

1. The text of this Appendix is transcribed from lectures given by the Author on July 12, 26, 28 and August 2, 1995 at the auditorium of the Brazilian Society for the Defense of Tradition, Family and Property. It has been updated and slightly revised.

- "And they [the angels] said to Lot: . . . all that are thine bring them out of this city, for we will destroy this place, because their cry [of their crimes] is grown loud before the Lord, who hath sent us to destroy them" (*Gen.* 19:12-13).
- "And they brought him forth, and set him without the city: and there they spoke to him, saying: Save thy life; look not back, neither stay thou in all the country about, but save thyself in the mountain, lest thou be also consumed" (*Gen.* 19:17).
- "And the Lord rained upon Sodom and Gomorrha brimstone and fire from the Lord out of heaven. And he destroyed these cities, and all the country about, all the inhabitants of the cities, and all things that spring from the earth. And his wife looking behind her, was turned into a statue of salt. And Abraham got up early in the morning, and . . . looked towards Sodom and Gomorrha, and the whole land of that country, and he saw the ashes rise up from the earth as the smoke of a furnace" (*Gen.* 19:24-28).
- "Thou shalt not lie with mankind as with womankind, because it is an abomination" (*Lev.* 18:22).
- "Defile not yourselves with any of these things [illicit unions, child sacrifice, sodomy, and bestiality] with which all the nations have been defiled, which I will cast out before you, and with which the land is defiled; the abominations of which I will visit, that it may vomit out its inhabitants. . . . Beware then, lest in like manner, it vomit you also out, if you do the like things" (*Lev.* 18:24-28).
- "If any one lie with a man as with a woman, both have committed an abomination, let them be put to death: their blood be upon them" (*Lev.* 20:13).
- "A woman shall not be clothed with man's apparel, neither shall a man use woman's apparel: for he that doeth these things is abominable before God" (*Deut.* 22:5).
- On the punishment that God prepared for the Jews: "And I will give children to be their princes, and the effeminate shall rule over them . . . the shew of their countenance hath answered them: and they have proclaimed abroad their sin as Sodom, and they have not hid it: woe to their souls, for evils are rendered to them. . . . The Lord standeth to judge the people" (*Is.* 3:4-13).

§ 3 In the ***New Testament***, Saint Paul indignantly castigates this vice against nature:

- "Do not err: neither fornicators, nor idolaters, nor adulterers, nor the effeminate, nor liers with mankind [sodomites] . . . shall possess the kingdom of God" (*1 Cor.* 6:9-10).
- In the *Epistle to the Romans*, the Apostle of the Gentiles threatens perverts with punishments even on this earth: "Wherefore God gave them up to the desires of their heart, unto uncleanness, to dishonor their own bodies among themselves. Who changed the truth of God into a lie; and worshipped and served the creature rather than the Creator, who is blessed for ever. Amen. For this cause God delivered them up to shameful affections. For their women have changed the natural use into that use which is against nature. And, in like manner, the men also, leaving the natural use of the women, have burned in their lusts one towards another, men with men working that which is filthy, and receiving in themselves the recompense which was due to their error" (*Rom.* 1:24-27).

How can one not relate the fulfillment of these threats to the AIDS epidemic now ravaging sodomites?

§ 4
- Saint Peter stresses the infamy of the sin of sodomy and the chastisement God reserves for it: "For if God . . . reducing the cities of the Sodomites, and of the Gomorrhites, into ashes, condemned them to be overthrown, making them an example to those that should after act wickedly, and delivered just Lot, oppressed by the injustice and lewd conversation of the wicked . . . [then] the Lord knoweth how to deliver the godly from temptation, but to reserve the unjust unto the day of judgment to be tormented" (*2 Peter* 2:4-9).

§ 5
- Saint Jude is no less severe: "As Sodom and Gomorrha, and the neighboring cities, in like manner, having given themselves to fornication, and going after other flesh, were made an example, suffering the punishment of eternal fire, in like manner these

men also defile the flesh, and despise dominion [of Christ], and blaspheme majesty" (*Jude* 7-8).[2]

The Tradition of the Ecclesiastical Magisterium

§ 6 The first statement of a Church council on homosexual practices was issued by the **Council of Elvira** (305-306). The decree excludes from communion, even *in articulo mortis* (at the moment of death), the *stupratores puerorum* (corrupters of boys).[3]

The decree of the **Council of Ancyra**, held in Asia Minor in 314, strongly influenced the Church of the West, and it was often cited as authoritative in later enactments against homosexual practices. Canon 17 speaks about those "who . . . commit [acts of] defilement with animals or males."[4] The Council of Ancyra established for these crimes a series of punishments according to the age and state of life the infractor:

"Those who have committed such crimes before age twenty, after fifteen years of penance, will be readmitted to the communion of prayer. Then, after remaining five years in that communion, let them receive the sacraments of oblation. However, let their lives be analyzed to establish how long a period of penance they should sustain in order

2. Vague references to sodomites, without special interest for our exposition, are found in *1 Tim.* 1:8-10. Other references to Sodom and Gomorrha, without express mention of the vice of homosexuality: *Deut.* 29:23; 32:32; *Jer.* 23:13-14; 49:18; 50:40; *Ezech.* 16:55-56; *Matt.* 10:15; *Rom.* 9:29; *Apoc.* 11:8.
3. *Concilium Illiberitarum*, in John J. McNeill, S.J., *The Church and the Homosexual* (Kansas City: Sheed Andrews and McMeel, Inc., 1976), p. 79 [cf. also John McNeill, *La Iglesia ante la homosexualidad* (Barcelona/Buenos Aires/Mexico: Grijalbo, 1979), p. 120].
4. *Concilium Ancyrense*, 16, 17; C. H. Turner, *Ecclesiae occidentalis monumenta iuris antiquissima*, Oxford, 1909, vol. XI, p. 19; on the influence of this Council, see *Capitulares Aquisgran*, (789), 48, Joannes Dominicus Mansi, XVIIb, col. 230; *Capitulare Caroli Magno*, 48, Mansi, XVIIb, col. 710; *Capitulare Caroli Magno et Ludovic*, 82, Mansi, XVIIb, col. 839; *Canones Isaac Episcopi Lingonensis*, 4, 11, Mansi, XVIIb, col. 1259; *Concilium Parisiensi*, (829), 1, 34, Mansi, XIV, col. 560, in J. McNeill, *ibid.*

to obtain mercy. For if they unrestrainedly gave themselves over to these crimes, let them devote more time to doing penance. However, those aged twenty and over and married who fall into these crimes, let them do penance for twenty-five years and [then] be received in the communion of prayer; and, remaining in it for five years, let them finally receive the sacraments of oblation. Moreover, if those who are married and over fifty years of age commit these crimes, let them obtain the grace of communion only at the end of their lives."[5]

§ 7 **Pope Saint Siricius** (384-399) issued norms for admission into the priestly state. They apply indirectly to homosexuality: "We deem it advisable to establish that, just as not everyone should be allowed to do a penance reserved for clerics, so also a layman should never be allowed to ascend to clerical honor after penance and reconciliation. Because although they have been purified of the contagion of all sins, those who formerly indulged in a multitude of vices should not receive the instruments to administer the Sacraments."[6]

§ 8 In the opening speech of the **XVI Council of Toledo** in 693, Egica, the Gothic King of Spain, exhorts the clergy to fight against homosexual practices: "See that you determine to extirpate that obscene crime committed by those who lie with males, whose fearful conduct defiles the charm of honest living and provokes from heaven the wrath of the Supreme Judge."[7]

§ 9 The most complete set of norms against homosexual practices in the medieval era is contained in the canons approved at the **Council of Naplouse**, assembled on January 23, 1120 under the direction of Garmund, Patriarch of Jerusalem, and Baldwin, King of the same city.[8] On that occasion, a sermon was preached about the evils that had befallen the Kingdom of Jerusalem. Earthquakes, plagues, and attacks by the Saracens were judged as a punishment from Heaven

---

5. See Council of Ancyra, in St. Peter Damian, *Liber Gomorrhianus*, in PL 145, cols. 172ff.
6. St. Siricius, *ibid.*, cols. 174f.
7. *Concilium Tolitanum*, 16, 3, Mansi, XII, col. 71, in J. McNeill, *op. cit.*, pp. 79-80.
8. *Concilium Neapolitanum* 8, Mansi, XXI, cols. 261-264, *ibid.*, p. 80.

for the sins of the people. As a consequence, the Council issued twenty-five canons against the sins of the flesh, four of which related to homosexual practices. Death at the stake was decreed for those convicted of those specific crimes.

§ 10 The **Third Lateran Council** (1179) establishes: "Anyone caught in the practice of the sin against nature, on account of which the wrath of God was unleashed upon the children of disobedience (*Eph.* 5:6), if he is a cleric, let him be demoted from his state and kept in reclusion in a monastery to do penance; if he is a layman, let him be excommunicated and kept rigorously distant from the communion of the faithful."[9]

§ 11 Such was the horror that surrounded the sin against nature that, by the late twelfth century, sodomy was a reserved sin for which absolution was reserved to the Pope and, in some cases, to the Bishop.[10]

§ 12 Nevertheless, with the Renaissance this vice surfaced again. Homosexuality was a matter of grave concern to **Saint Pius V**. As well-known historian von Pastor narrates, "In the first year of his pontificate, the Pope had two preponderant concerns: zeal for the Inquisition and the struggle against 'this horrendous sin whereby the justice of God caused the cities contaminated by it to be consumed in flames.' On April 1, 1566, he ordered that sodomites be turned over to the secular arm. . . . The various imprisonments of sodomites . . . impressed Rome and frightened especially well-established people, for it was known that the Pope wanted his laws enforced even against the powerful. Indeed, to punish for vices against nature, the torment of the stake was applied throughout the pontificate of Saint Pius V. . . . An earlier papal Brief mandated that clerics who were guilty of that

---

9. *Concilium Lateranense can. 11*, Mansi, XXII, cols. 224ff., in Fabio Bernadei, *Chiesa e omosessualità—la ragioni di un'immutabili condanna* (Rome: Centro Culturale Lepanto, 1995), p. 13.
10. *Synodus constitutiva Odonis episcopi Parisiensi* (1196), 4, 5—Pope and Bishop: Mansi XXIII, col. 678; *Concilium Provinciale Fritzlar* (1287), 4—Bishop: Mansi, XXIII, col 726; *Sancta Synodus ecclesiae Leodicae* (1287), 4—Bishop: Mansi, XXIV, col. 891; *Concilium Ramense* (1408), Mansi, XXVI, col. 1073, in J. McNeill, *op. cit.*, p. 80.

crime be stripped of all their posts, dignities, and income, and, after degradation, be handed over to the secular arm."[11]

The Holy Inquisitor promulgated two Constitutions in which he castigates and punishes the sin against nature.

In the Constitution ***Cum Primum*** of April 1, 1566, Saint Pius V solemnly established: "Having set our minds to remove everything that may in some way offend the Divine Majesty, We resolve to punish, above all and without indulgence, those things which, by the authority of the Sacred Scriptures or by most grievous examples, are most repugnant to God and elicit His wrath; that is, negligence in divine worship, ruinous simony, the crime of blasphemy, and the execrable libidinous vice against nature. For which faults peoples and nations are scourged by God, according to His just condemnation, with catastrophes, wars, famine and plagues. . . . Let the judges know that, if even after this, Our Constitution, they are negligent in punishing these crimes, they will be guilty of them at Divine Judgment and will also incur Our indignation. . . . If someone commits that nefarious crime against nature that caused divine wrath to be unleashed against the children of iniquity, he will be given over to the secular arm for punishment; and if he is a cleric, he will be subject to analogous punishment after having been stripped of all his degrees [of ecclesiastical dignity]."[12]

Saint Pius V is no less rigorous in the Constitution ***Horrendum Illud Scelus*** of August 30, 1568. He teaches: "That horrible crime, on account of which corrupt and obscene cities were burned by virtue of divine condemnation, causes Us most bitter sorrow and shocks Our mind, impelling it to repress such a crime with the highest possible zeal. Quite opportunely the **Fifth Lateran Council** [1512-1517] decrees: Let any member of the clergy caught in that vice against nature . . . be removed from the clerical order or forced to do penance in a monastery (chap. 4, X, V, 31).

"So that the contagion of such a grave offense may not advance

11. Ludovico von Pastor, *Historia de los Papas* (Barcelona: Gustavo Gili, 1931), vol. XVII, pp. 299f.
12. St. Pius V, Constitution *Cum Primum*, April 1, 1566, in *Bullarium Romanum* (Rome: Typographia Reverendae Camerae Apostolicae, Mainardi,1738), vol. IV, chap. II, p. 284, in F. Bernadei, *op. cit.*, p. 14.

with greater audacity, taking advantage of impunity, which is the greatest incitement to sin, and so as to more severely punish the clerics who are guilty of this nefarious crime and who are not frightened by the death of their souls, We determine that they should be handed over to the secular authority, which enforces civil law. Therefore, wishing to pursue with the greatest rigor that which We have decreed since the beginning of Our Pontificate, We establish that any priest or member of the clergy, either secular or regular, who commits such an execrable crime, by force of the present law be deprived of every clerical privilege, of every post, dignity and ecclesiastical benefit, and having been degraded by an ecclesiastical judge, be immediately delivered to the secular authority to be executed as mandated by law, according to the appropriate punishment for laymen plunged in this abyss."[13]

§ 13 The **Code of Canon Law** undertaken at the initiative and encouragement of **Saint Pius X**, and published in 1917 by his successor **Pope Benedict XV**, says this: "So far as laymen are concerned, the sin of sodomy is punished *ipso facto* with the pain of *infamy* and other sanctions to be applied according to the prudent judgment of the Bishop depending on the gravity of each case (*Can.* 2357). As for ecclesiastics and religious, if they are *clerici minoris* [that is, of a degree lower than deacon], let them be punished with various measures, proportional to the gravity of the fault, that can even include dismissal from the clerical state (*Can.* 2358); if they are *clerici maiores* [that is, deacons, priests or bishops], let them 'be declared *infamous* and suspended from every post, benefit, dignity, deprived of their eventual stipend and, in the gravest cases, let them be deposed' (*Can.* 2359, par. 2)."[14]

* * *

§ 14 **Tertullian**, the great apologist of the Church in the second century, writes: "All other frenzies of lusts which exceed the laws of nature and are impious toward both bodies and the sexes we banish

---

13. St. Pius V, Constitution *Horrendum Illud Scelus*, August 30, 1568, *ibid.*, chap. III, p. 33.
14. Benedict XV, *Code of Canon Law*, *ibid.*, p. 16.

. . . from all shelter of the Church, for they are not sins so much as monstrosities."[15]

§ 15 **Saint Basil of Caesarea**, the fourth century Church Father who wrote the principal rule of the monks of the East, establishes this: "The cleric or monk who molests youths or boys or is caught kissing or committing some turpitude, let him be whipped in public, deprived of his crown [tonsure] and, after having his head shaved, let his face be covered with spittle; and [let him be] bound in iron chains, condemned to six months in prison, reduced to eating rye bread once a day in the evening three times per week. After these six months living in a separate cell under the custody of a wise elder with great spiritual experience, let him be subjected to prayers, vigils and manual work, always under the guard of two spiritual brothers, without being allowed to have any relationship . . . with young people."[16]

§ 16 **Saint Augustine** is categorical in the combat against sodomy and similar vices. The great Bishop of Hippo writes: "Sins against nature, therefore, like the sin of Sodom, are abominable and deserve punishment whenever and wherever they are committed. If all nations committed them, all alike would be held guilty of the same charge in God's law, for our Maker did not prescribe that we should use each other in this way. In fact, the relationship that we ought to have with God is itself violated when our nature, of which He is Author, is desecrated by perverted lust."[17]

Further on he reiterates: "Your punishments are for the sins which men commit against themselves, because, although they sin against You, they do wrong in their own souls and their malice is self-betrayed. They corrupt and pervert their own nature, which You made and for which You shaped the rules, either by making wrong use of the things which You allow, or by becoming inflamed with passion 'to make unnatural use of things which You do not allow' (*Rom.* 1:26)."[18]

---

15. Tertullian, *De pudicitia*, IV, in J. McNeill, *op. cit.*, p. 89.
16. St. Basil of Caesarea, in St. Peter Damien, *Liber Gomorrhianus, op. cit.*, cols. 174f.
17. St. Augustine, *Confessions* (New York: Penguin, 1967), Book III, chap. 8, p. 65.
18. *Ibid.*, p. 66.

§ 17 **Saint John Chrysostom** denounces homosexual acts as being contrary to nature. Commenting on the *Epistle to the Romans* (1:26-27), he says that the pleasures of sodomy are an unpardonable offense to nature and are doubly destructive, since they threaten the species by deviating the sexual organs away from their primary procreative end and they sow disharmony between men and women, who no longer are inclined by physical desire to live together in peace.[19]

The brilliant Patriarch of Constantinople employs most severe words for the vice we are analyzing. Saint John Chrysostom makes this strong argument: "All passions are dishonorable, for the soul is even more prejudiced and degraded by sin than is the body by disease; but the worst of all passions is lust between men. . . . The sins against nature are more difficult and less rewarding, so much so that one cannot even say that they procure pleasure, since true pleasure is only the one according to nature. But when God abandons a man, everything is turned upside down! Therefore, not only are their passions [of the homosexuals] satanic, but their lives are diabolic. . . . So I say to you that these are even worse than murderers, and that it would be better to die than to live in such dishonor. A murderer only separates the soul from the body, whereas these destroy the soul inside the body. . . . There is nothing, absolutely nothing more mad or damaging than this perversity."[20]

§ 18 **Saint Gregory the Great** delves deeper into the symbolism of the fire and brimstone that God used to punish the sodomites: "Brimstone calls to mind the foul odors of the flesh, as Sacred Scripture itself confirms when it speaks of the rain of fire and brimstone poured by the Lord upon Sodom. He had decided to punish in it the crimes of the flesh, and the very type of punishment emphasized the shame of that crime, since brimstone exhales stench and fire burns. It was, therefore, just that the sodomites, burning with perverse desires that originated from the foul odor of flesh, should perish at the same time by fire and brimstone so that through this just chastisement they

19. St. John Chrysostom, *In Epistulam ad Romanos IV*, in J. McNeill, *op. cit.*, pp. 89-90.
20. St. John Chrysostom, *Homilia in Epistula Pauli ad Romanos*, in PG 47, cols. 360ff., in F. Bernadei, *op. cit.* pp. 7f.

might realize the evil perpetrated under the impulse of a perverse desire."[21]

§ 19 **Saint Peter Damian**'s *Liber Gomorrhianus* [Book of Gomorrha], addressed to Pope Leo IX in the year 1051, is considered the principal work against homosexuality.[22] It reads: "Just as Saint Basil establishes that those who incur sins [against nature] . . . should be subjected not only to a hard penance but a public one, and Pope Siricius prohibits penitents from entering clerical orders, one can clearly deduce that he who corrupts himself with a man through the ignominious squalor of a filthy union does not deserve to exercise ecclesiastical functions, since those who were formerly given to vices . . . become unfit to administer the Sacraments."[23]

§ 20 **Saint Albert the Great** gives four reasons why he considers homosexual acts as the most detestable ones: They are born from an ardent frenzy; they are disgustingly foul; those who become addicted to them are seldom freed from that vice; they are as contagious as disease, passing quickly from one person to another.[24]

§ 21 **Saint Thomas Aquinas**, writing about sins against nature, explains: "However, they are called passions of ignominy because they are not worthy of being named, according to that passage in *Ephesians* (5:12): 'For the things that are done by them in secret, it is a shame even to speak of.' For if the sins of the flesh are commonly censurable because they lead man to that which is bestial in him, much more so is the sin against nature, by which man debases himself lower than even his animal nature."[25]

---

21. St. Gregory the Great, *Commento morale a Giobbe* (Rome: Città Nuova, 1994), XIV, 23, vol. II, p. 371, *Ibid.*, p. 7.
22. J. McNeill, *op. cit.*, p. 80.
23. St. Peter Damian, *op. cit.*, cols. 174f.
24. St. Albert the Great, *In Evangelium Lucae XVII*, 29, in J. McNeill, *op. cit.*, p. 95.
25. St. Thomas Aquinas, *Super Epistulas Sancti Pauli Ad Romanum* I, 26, pp. 27f.

§ 22 **Saint Bonaventure**, speaking in a sermon at the church of Saint Mary of Portiuncula about the miracles that took place simultaneously with the birth of Our Lord Jesus Christ, narrates this: "Seventh prodigy: All sodomites—men and women—died all over the earth, as Saint Jerome said in his commentary on the psalm 'The light was born for the just.' This made it clear that He was born to reform nature and promote chastity."[26]

§ 23 **Saint Catherine of Siena**, a religious mystic of the 14th century, relays words of Our Lord Jesus Christ about the vice against nature, which contaminated part of the clergy in her time. Referring to sacred ministers, He says: "They not only fail from resisting this frailty [of fallen human nature] . . . but do even worse as they commit the cursed sin against nature. Like the blind and stupid, having dimmed the light of their understanding, they do not recognize the disease and misery in which they find themselves. For this not only causes Me nausea, but displeases even the demons themselves, whom these miserable creatures have chosen as their lords. For Me, this sin against nature is so abominable that, for it alone, five cities were submersed, by virtue of the judgment of My Divine Justice, which could no longer bear them. . . . It is disagreeable to the demons, not because evil displeases them and they find pleasure in good, but because their nature is angelic and thus is repulsed upon seeing such an enormous sin being committed. It is true that it is the demon who hits the sinner with the poisoned arrow of lust, but when a man carries out such a sinful act, the demon leaves."[27]

§ 24 **Saint Bernardine of Siena**, a preacher of the fifteenth century, makes an accurate psychological analysis of the consequences of the homosexual vice. The illustrious Franciscan writes: "No sin has greater power over the soul than the one of cursed sodomy, which was always detested by all those who lived according to God. . . . Such passion for undue forms borders on madness. This vice disturbs the intellect, breaks an elevated and generous state of soul, drags

26. St. Bonaventure, *Sermon XXI—In Nativitate Domini*, in *Catolicismo* (Campos/São Paulo), December 1987, p. 3; F. Bernadei, *op. cit.*, p. 11.
27. St. Catherine of Siena, *El diálogo*, in *Obras de Santa Catarina de Siena* (Madrid: BAC, 1991), p. 292.

great thoughts to petty ones, makes [men] pusillanimous and irascible, obstinate and hardened, servilely soft and incapable of anything. Furthermore, the will, being agitated by the insatiable drive for pleasure, no longer follows reason, but furor. . . . Someone who lived practicing the vice of sodomy will suffer more pains in Hell than anyone else, because this is the worst sin that there is."[28]

§ 25 **Saint Peter Canisius** says this about the sin of sodomy: "Those who are not ashamed of violating divine and natural law are slaves of this turpitude that can never be sufficiently execrated."[29]

§ 26 Prof. **Plinio Corrêa de Oliveira**, in an SBT interview about homosexuality in Brazil (not broadcast) on October 29, 1992, stated: "The sexual act exists in the natural order of things for the fecundity of the family and, through the fecundity of the family, for the expansion of mankind. The precept of Our Lord Jesus Christ to men . . . is 'Multiply and fill the earth.' It is necessary, therefore, to do this and by all means to favor the fecundity of sexual intercourse, which is legitimately exercised only in Matrimony. Now then, as for homosexuality, there is no Matrimony, and, above all, there can be no fecundity. . . .

"For many centuries," Prof. Corrêa de Oliveira continued, "homosexuality was the object of real aversion on the part of successive generations. And this was not because of a whim . . . but by virtue of the doctrinal principles I have just enunciated, which are principles of the Roman Catholic and Apostolic doctrine. . . . This rejection [of homosexuality] is a preservation of society against that which of itself threatens it. Everything that is alive rejects what destroys it. Thus, by a similar movement of the instinct of self-preservation, human societies modeled upon Catholic doctrine . . . have been profoundly anti-homosexual."

Question: "Why, in your view, are homosexuals discriminated against in Brazilian society?"

---

28. St. Bernardine of Siena, *Predica XXXIX*, in *Le prediche volgari* (Milan: Rizzoli, 1936), pp. 869ff., 915, in F. Bernadei, *op. cit.*, pp. 11f.
29. St. Peter Canisius, *Summa Doctrina Christianae*, III, a, b (Cooniae, Colenium, 1557), p. 455, *ibid.*, p. 12.

Answer: "Brazil is a son of Portugal, and Portugal and Spain were always very strong bulwarks of the Catholic Church. We received from our Portuguese ancestors rigidity and consistency in the Catholic Faith, which was the model for the customs of colonial Brazil, the United Kingdom [of Brazil and Portugal], the Brazilian Empire and the Brazilian Republic until some time ago. Hence Catholic aversion for homosexuality impregnated our customs and constituted a tradition."

The Tradition of Civil Legislation

§ 27 In civil as well as religious law, there is a tradition of intolerance for the sin of homosexuality.

Law of December 16, 342 of **Emperors Constantius** and **Constans** that was included in the later *Theodosian Code*: "When a man marries and is ready to offer himself to men in a feminine way [*quum vir nubit in feminam viris porrecturam*] . . . We order that norms be established, that the law be armed with an avenging sword, and that these infamous persons . . . receive the supreme punishment."[30]

Law of August 6, 390 promulgated by the **Emperors Valentian II, Theodosius,** and **Arcadius:** "All persons having the shameful custom of condemning a man's body to play the role of a woman . . . (for they seem not to be different from women) shall expiate this type of crime in avenging flames before the public."[31]

Law of December 30, 533 of **Emperor Justinian:** "In cases of penal suits, public prosecution will be guided by various statutes, including the *Law Julia de Adulteris* . . . that punishes with death [*gladio*] not only those who violate the marriages of others, but also those who commit acts of vile concupiscence with other men."[32]

Law of the year 538 of Emperor Justinian: "Whereas certain men, overcome by diabolical incitement to practice among themselves the

---

30. *Codex Theodosii,* IX; VIII, 3.
31. *Ibid.*, IX. VII. 6.
32. Justinian, *Corpus Iuris Civilis*, Institutes IV. xviii. 4.

most unworthy lewdness and acts contrary to nature, we exhort them to be fearful of God and the coming judgment, and to abstain from such illicit and diabolical practices so that the just wrath of God may not fall upon them on account of these heathen acts, with the result that cities perish with all their inhabitants. For Sacred Scriptures teach us that similar impious acts caused the demise of cities with all their inhabitants. . . .

"#1. And since such sins are the cause of famine, earthquakes, and plagues, we warn men to abstain from these acts so as not to lose their souls. But if, after this warning of ours, it should be discovered that any persist in such iniquity, they render themselves unworthy of God's mercy and further will be subjected to the punishment established by law.

"#2. Thus we order the most illustrious Prefect of the Capital to arrest those who persist in the aforesaid illicit and impious acts after they have been warned by us, and to inflict upon them the most severe punishments, so that the city and the State do not end by suffering on account of such iniquitous acts."[33]

The influence of the *Justinian Code* continued for centuries. It can still be noted in Blackstone's *Comment on the Laws of England* in the nineteenth century. Blackstone states: "The crime against nature . . . [is one which] . . . the voice of nature and of reason, and the express law of God, determined to be capital. Of which we have a special instance, long before the Jewish dispensation, in the destruction of two cities by fire from heaven; so that this is a universal, not merely a provincial, precept. In the *Old Testament* the law condemns sodomists (and possibly other homosexual offenders) to death as perpetrators of an abomination against the Lord, while in the *New Testament*, they are denounced as transgressors of the natural order and are disinherited from the kingdom of God as followers of the vile practices of the heathens."[34]

Jurist Pietro Agostino d'Avack drafted an historic roster of laws that protected the State against the vice of homosexuality. In substantial paragraphs, d'Avack affirms: "No less severe and scathingly repressive laws against such sexual aberrations are found in the cen-

---

33. Justinian, *Novel* 77 [358 CE].
34. Blackstone, *Comment on the Laws of England*, London, 1826, vol. IV, p. 215, *op. cit.* McNeill, p. 78.

turies following [the Roman Empire] and emanated from all civil authorities from the earliest medieval times up to the modern age. Thus, the *Lex Visigothica* condemned to castration and jail those [men] 'who carnally united with men. . . .' and prescribed, if they were married, that their goods should be immediately inherited by their children and heirs. After the *castratio virum*, the law also prescribed capital punishment.

"In turn, in the well-known collection of the *Frankish Capitularies of Ansegisius and Benedict Levite* . . . those who had engaged in sexual acts with animals, who were guilty of incest and who 'practiced copulation with men' were punished with capital punishment; if pardoned by some indult, they were obliged to subject themselves to the canonical penances imposed by the Church. In the later *Capitularies of Ludovicus Pius*, while such a crime, invoking Roman legislation, was punishable with execution at the stake, this severe action was justified in the name of the 'salvation of the *rem publicam* (nation)' so that 'on account of such sins, we may not also fall with the kingdom and the glory of the whole kingdom may not perish.'. . .

"During successive centuries, this lay civil legislation was substantially unaltered and was nearly identical everywhere, whether in Italy or in the other European States, as attested to by the *Statutes of Bologna* in 1561, those of Ferrara in 1566, those of Milan, Rome and [the Italian province of] Marche in the seventeenth century, the *Florentian Tires* of 1542, 1558 and 1699, the *Sicilian Pragmatics* of 1504, the *Carolingean Criminal Constitution* of Charles V, the *Theresian* [*Constitution*] of Marie Thérèse, the *Royal Portuguese Ordination*, the *New Spanish Recompilation,* etc. . . . For their part, the *Florentian Statutes*, 'execrating the indecency of the great crime that is the sodomite vice and wishing to extirpate it,' approved the institution of eight *officiales honestatis* (officers of decency) who were designated for six months specifically to repress such crime."[35]

2. THE POST-CONCILIAR TEACHING ON HOMOSEXUALITY

§ 28 The principles of adaptation of the Church to the modern world

35. Pietro Agostino d'Avack, "L'omosessualità nel Diritto Canonico," in *Ulisse*, Spring of 1953, pp. 682-685, in F. Bernadei, *op. cit*., pp. 21f.

approved by the Council, as well as the general acceptance of tolerance and mercy as remedies for evil, had a special application in the case of homosexuality.

Modern psychology is divided into various currents with respect to this vice. One current believes that homosexuality results from the influence of various environmental factors—family troubles, emotional imbalance of the mother, bad example, etc. Others opine that it is due to innate factors—the simultaneous presence of masculine and feminine genes in the constitution of homosexuals, or a certain number of brain cells that determine homosexuality.

For a considerable segment of modern psychologists, homosexuality does not result from a person's concession to an unnatural tendency nor is it a moral vice; on the contrary, it is something according to nature, or at worst simply an illness, which should be accepted as normal.

Conciliar Principles of Adaptation and Tolerance

§ 29 With its general rule of adaptation to the modern world, the Council had to adapt to its theories. Insofar as modern psychology is concerned, it declares in the Constitution ***Gaudium et Spes***:

- "Advances in . . . psychology and the social sciences not only lead man to greater self-awareness, but provide him with the technical means of molding the lives of whole peoples as well." (GS 5b)
- "Recent psychological advances furnish deeper insights into human behavior." (GS 54a)
- "Let the faithful incorporate the findings of new sciences and teachings and the understanding of the most recent discoveries with Christian morality and thought, so that their practice of religion and their moral behavior may keep abreast of their acquaintance with science and of the relentless progress of technology." (GS 62f)
- "In pastoral care, sufficient use should be made, not only of theological principles, but also of the findings of secular sciences, especially psychology and sociology." (GS 62b)

§ 30 With respect to tolerance for the errors and moral evils afflicting the world, in the *Opening Speech* of the first session of Vatican II, **Pope John XXIII** declared: "The Church has always opposed these errors. Frequently she has condemned them with the greatest severity. Nowadays, however, the Spouse of Christ prefers to make use of the medicine of mercy rather than that of severity. She considers that she meets the needs of the present day by demonstrating the validity of her teaching rather than by condemnations . . . That being so, the Catholic Church, raising the torch of religious truth by means of this Ecumenical Council, desires to show herself to be the loving mother of all, benign, patient, full of mercy and goodness toward the brethren who are separated from her."[36]

Such principles led to the acceptance of modern psychology's theories about homosexuality, and also to the tolerance the Church has manifested since then toward this vice.

Documents of the Holy See on Homosexuality

§ 31 As far as we can see, there are three basic documents of the Holy See on the question of homosexuality. They are all from the Congregation for the Doctrine of the Faith.

In order to understand these documents well, it seems appropriate for us to make some preliminary observations.

Up until Vatican Council II, the language of ecclesiastical documents was habitually clear and accessible, continuing the line of coherence of the Magisterium through the centuries. The body of doctrine thus being built constituted a supremely true, good and beautiful ensemble, a worthy reflection of Our Lord Jesus Christ, the Incarnate Wisdom.

After Vatican II, however, ecclesiastical language often forsook such characteristics. Now more, now less, we find in it the presence of two opposing currents of thought: the traditional doctrine of the Church and progressivism. For this reason, often a text can lend itself to different and even contradictory interpretations—a lamentable but obvious fact

36. John XXIII, Opening Speech of Vatican Council II, October 11, 1962, in Walter M. Abbott, S.J., General Editor, *The Document of Vatican II* (New York: Guild Press, 1966), p. 716.

to someone who has any experience reading post-conciliar documents.

This fact necessitates establishing a method of analysis that permits us to confidently discern the depth of progressivist thought present in the text and the gates it thus opens for error and evil.

The method we use is to determine that which is most unusual in each document and analyze it in order to build an overall picture.

We know that more often than not there is a possible conservative interpretation for other excerpts of the documents. We leave this aside, for it seems to us more consonant with the spirit of Catholic vigilance to pay more attention to evil, which invades with its characteristic impact, rather than to good, which is often content to survive, impassive and silent, this invasion.

Based upon these premises, therefore, we go on to analyze the three documents of the Congregation for the Doctrine of the Faith.

§ 32 Dated December 29, 1975, the **first document** is entitled *Declaration on Certain Questions Concerning Sexual Ethics*, signed by Cardinal Franjo Seper and approved by Pope Paul VI. In our view, so far as homosexuality is concerned, the document's words tore down the barrier of horror that held back the waters of this vice against nature. In the document, Cardinal Seper says:

"At the present time there are those who, basing themselves on observations in the psychological order, have begun to judge indulgently, and even to excuse completely, homosexual relations between certain people. This they do in opposition to the constant teaching of the Magisterium and to the moral sense of the Christian people.

"A distinction is drawn, and it seems with some reason, between homosexuals whose tendency comes from a false education, from a lack of normal sexual development, from habit, from bad example, or from other similar causes, and is transitory or at least not incurable; and homosexuals who are definitively such because of some kind of innate instinct or a pathological constitution judged to be incurable.

"In regard to this second category of subjects, some people conclude that their tendency is so natural that it justifies in their case homosexual relations within a sincere communion of life and love analogous to marriage, in so far as such homosexuals feel incapable of enduring a solitary life.

"In the pastoral field,[37] these homosexuals must certainly be treated with understanding and sustained in the hope of overcoming their personal difficulties and their inability to fit into society. Their culpability will be judged with prudence. But no pastoral method can be employed which would give moral justification to these acts on the grounds that they would be consonant with the condition of such people. For according to the objective moral order, homosexual relations are acts which lack an essential and indispensable finality. In Sacred Scripture they are condemned as a serious depravity and even presented as the sad consequence of rejecting God. (*Rom.* 1:24-27; cf. also *1 Cor.* 6:10, *1 Tim.* 1:10). This judgment of Scripture does not of course permit us to conclude that all those who suffer from this anomaly are personally responsible for it, but it does attest to the fact that homosexual acts are intrinsically disordered and can in no case be approved."[38]

One sees, therefore, that Cardinal Seper distinguishes between an objective moral order—that should theoretically be respected—and a subjective moral order that should orient the pastoral action of the Church, which in some cases should accept homosexuality as a *fait accompli*. Note that on implicitly assuming the erroneous premises of modern psychology to justify Church pastoral action, Cardinal Seper provides a powerful theoretical argument opposed to objective Catholic morals, which he sought to defend.

Further on, the Cardinal, enunciating general principles that should govern questions related to homosexuality, pre-matrimonial relations, and masturbation, states: "It is true that in sins of sexual order, in view of their kind and their causes, it more easily happens that free consent is not fully given; this is a fact which calls for caution in all judgment as to the subject's responsibility."[39]

---

37. With regard to the tendency of "pastoral activity" to become a doctrinal reality, the Reader can consult the interesting opinion of Prof. Fernand Dumont in Chap. VI § 115 above. According to this author, pastoral theology would gradually but definitively replace dogmatic theology.
38. Congregation for the Doctrine of the Faith, *Declaration on Certain Questions Concerning Sexual Ethics* of December 29, 1975 (Washington: United States Catholic Conference, 1976), no. 8, pp. 8-9.
39. *Ibid.*, p. 12, n. 10.

These were the principles that, in a certain way, legitimized and gave free rein to homosexuality in the Church. While this vice had already surfaced to the light of day on the basis of conciliar *aggiornamento*, only after the publication of this document did it feel at ease.

Ten years went by before the Holy See felt the need for a new pronouncement in face of the veritable homosexual avalanche that had fallen upon the contemporary world. However, in dealing with the topic, the point of reference was the document of 1975.[40]

§ 33 We add here a short observation to aid in the reading of the documents below.

In them, Cardinal Ratzinger does not seem to be very precise in distinguishing between two fundamental concepts: homosexual tendency (or inclination or orientation) and homosexual behavior.

According to Catholic doctrine, any disordered tendency, above all toward a vice contrary to nature, cannot have the right to exist in a person's thoughts. If someone in his mind makes a concession to this tendency, he sins. This is why in the *Confiteor* one asks forgiveness for sins of thought, word and deed. Thus, a homosexual tendency is not a sin only when it has not been at all willed or accepted by the person.

A person also sins when he outwardly expresses a homosexual tendency. Indeed, we have seen excerpts from Sacred Scripture (*Deut.* 22:5; *Is.* 3:4-13) and from Saint Basil prescribing severe punishment for those who behave in a homosexual fashion ("kissing or committing some turpitude") even though they do not practice the act.

Finally, there is the act of sodomy, which constitutes a sin that cries out to Heaven and clamors to God for vengeance.[41]

Yet such clear and precise concepts of tendency, behavior and act

---

40. For example: Congregazione Per L'Educazione Cattolica, *Orientamenti educativi sull'amore umano*, November 1, 1983, Poliglota Vaticana, pp. 32f., nn. 101ff.
41. *Gen.* 19:13; St. Pius X, *The Catechism of Pope Saint Pius X*, extracted from *A Compendium of Catechetical Instruction*, Msgr. John Hagen, ed., 1910 (Gladysdale, Vic.: Instauratio Press, 1993), p. 174; Rev. Francis Spirago; Rev. Richard F. Clarke, S.J., ed., *The Catechism Explained* (New York: Benziger, 1899; Rockford: TAN, 1993), p. 461; F. X. Schouppe, *Curso abreviado de Religião ou verdade e beleza da Religião Cristã* (Porto: Liv. Chardron, 1875), p. 296.

with regard to sodomy are somewhat shuffled around in the documents we are examining.

At times in these documents, the tendency remains in the individual's thoughts; at other times, it manifests itself and is confused with behavior. The concept of behavior is uncertain as well. At times, it is a public manifestation of homosexuality without practicing the act; at other times it includes the act.

Perhaps this confusion can be explained as follows: Since the homosexual act is indisputably sinful but the tendency is not categorically so, emphasizing the notion of tendency would be the shrewd thing to do by someone who wants to morally justify homosexual behavior.

The word "tendency" is also taken as synonymous with "inclination," and the word "behavior" is replaced by homosexual "practice" or "activity."

Having clarified these imprecisions as much as possible, we will proceed to the analysis of the document.

§ 34 On October 1, 1986, the Congregation for the Doctrine of the Faith published its **second document** on the subject. It was called *Letter to the Bishops of the Catholic Church on the Pastoral Care of Homosexual Persons*, signed by Joseph Cardinal Ratzinger and approved by Pope John Paul II. The document was prepared with the intention of repressing abuses taking place in debates about homosexuality, even in Catholic ambiences,[42] as well as correcting "an overly benign interpretation" to "the homosexual condition itself" which some had given to the prior document of the Holy See on homosexuality (n. 3).

To this end, Cardinal Ratzinger distinguishes between homosexual tendency and behavior:

"Although the particular inclination of the homosexual person is not a sin, it is a more or less strong tendency ordered toward an intrinsic moral evil; and thus the inclination itself must be seen as an objective disorder" (n. 3).

---

42. Congregazione Per La Dottrina Della Fede, "Lettera ai Vescovi della Chiesa Cattolica sulla cura pastorale delle persone omosessuali" of October 1, 1986, in *L'Osservatore Romano*, 10/31/1986, p. 5, n. 1.

Cardinal Ratzinger says that the act is intrinsically evil and that the inclination is objectively disordered without being a sin properly speaking. This is in accordance with Catholic doctrine.

The Cardinal also states: "Homosexual activity is not a complementary union, able to transmit life; and so it thwarts the call to a life of that form of self-giving which the Gospel says is the essence of Christian living. This does not mean that homosexual persons are not often generous and giving of themselves; but when they engage in homosexual activity they confirm within themselves a disordered sexual inclination which is essentially self-indulgent" (n. 7).

Thus, on affirming certain current principles of moral teaching, the Prefect of the Congregation for the Doctrine of the Faith begins to praise homosexuals: They are often generous and giving of themselves. This makes it appear as if he were seeking legitimacy for them.

This hypothesis is more strongly confirmed in the text below, in which he writes: "It is deplorable that homosexual persons have been and are the object of violent malice in speech or in action. Such treatment deserves condemnation from the Church's pastors wherever it occurs. It reveals a kind of disregard for others which endangers the most fundamental principles of a healthy society. The intrinsic dignity of each person must always be respected in word, in action and in law" (n. 10).

Note that Cardinal Ratzinger thus advocates legislation defending homosexuals from lack of respect, that is, violent malice in speech or in action.

Overall, one may say of this Instruction of the Holy See that although on the one hand it condemns the homosexual act as entirely evil from the moral standpoint, on the other hand it defends homosexuals who openly declare themselves as such but do not practice the homosexual act.

§ 35 On July 24, 1992, *L'Osservatore Romano* published the **third document** of the same Congregation on the subject, entitled "Some Considerations concerning the Catholic Response to Legislative Proposals on the Non-Discrimination of Homosexual Persons." (June, 1992). It is addressed to the Bishops of the United States but is undated. Its foreword says that the published version is a second draft written after consultation with the Bishops. More atypically, it

says that the considerations in the document are not intended as an official instruction, but only as a resource for "the conscientious Catholic legislator, voter, or Church authority who is confronted with such issues."[43]

Its objective, therefore, is to orient the Bishops on what position to take regarding civil laws protecting homosexuals. That is to say, the boldest request made in the prior document becomes the premise of this one.

The document, published on the authority of Cardinal Ratzinger, says: "Homosexual persons, as human persons, have the same rights as all persons, including that of not being treated in a manner which offends their personal dignity. Among other rights, all persons have the right to work, to housing, etc. Nevertheless, these rights are not absolute. They can be legitimately limited for objectively disordered external conduct" (n. 12).

It had earlier declared: "There are areas in which it is not unjust discrimination to take sexual orientation[44] into account, for example, in the consignment of children to adoption or foster care, in employment of teachers or coaches, and in military recruitment" (n. 11).

Further on, he makes a prudential warning: "Including 'homosexual orientation' among the considerations on the basis of which it is illegal to discriminate can easily lead to regarding homosexuality as a positive source of human rights . . . The passage from the recognition of homosexuality as a factor on which basis it is illegal to discriminate can easily lead, if not automatically, to the legislative protection of homosexuality" (n. 13). Thus, it would not be advisable to take homosexuality as the basis for a legal right.

In its whole, the document advocates that homosexuals be recognized as having rights on the basis of being human persons, but not on the basis of homosexuality. A certain contradiction remains in its concept of tendency or orientation. At times, orientation is taken to

---

43. Congregazione per la Dottrina Della Fede, "Alcune considerazioni concernenti la risposta a proposte di legge sulla non-discriminazione delle persone omosessuali," in *L'Osservatore Romano*, 7/24/1992, p. 4.
44. The document presents a definition of "orientation": "An individual's sexual orientation is generally not known to others unless he publicly identifies himself as having this orientation or unless some overt behavior manifests it" (n. 14).

mean an inclination that is not manifested publicly, and at times as something that is perceived and may or may not be subject to a law.

Finally, in the document there are two notions of discrimination against homosexuals. One it calls unjust, allegedly coming from a lack of respect for human rights. Another is just, but it is ambiguous because it derives from the concept of homosexual orientation. This just discrimination only becomes clear in the case of the examples given—the adoption of children, choosing teachers or physical educators, and in the military service.

§ 36 A characteristic application of this ambiguity in the concept of homosexual tendency can be found in the short Allocution delivered by **Pope John Paul II** on the occasion of the approval of "marriage" of homosexuals by the European Parliament. Indeed, he says: "Our thought turns toward the recent and well-known resolution approved by the European Parliament. In it, they do not simply limit themselves to the defense of persons with homosexual tendencies, refusing to allow unjust discriminations toward them. On this point, the Church is also in agreement, approves it, and makes it her own, since every human person is worthy of respect. What is morally inadmissible is the juridical approval of homosexual practice."[45]

Summarizing the concessions made, we have the following:

§ 37

- In the *first document* Cardinal Seper admits that there seems to be some foundation to the theories of modern psychology which claim that in some cases homosexuality is part of the person's psychic makeup and hence judged to be incurable.
- In the name of pastoral care, he recommends that the Church's attitude toward homosexuals be one of understanding and encouragement toward overcoming their problems.
- He says that those who "suffer from this anomaly" are not necessarily "personally responsible for it."

---

45. John Paul II, Allocution of the Angelus, February 20, 1994, published under the title "Con la risoluzione del Parlamento Europeo si è chiesto di legittimare un disordine morale," in *L'Osservatore Romano*, 2/21-22/1994, pp. 1, 5.

- He says that sexual faults are more easily committed without full consent, and hence one must be prudent in passing judgment on the subjective culpability of the one who commits such faults.

§ 38
- In the *second document* Cardinal Ratzinger calls for condemnation of violent malice in speech or in action against homosexuals; also, based on human dignity, he calls for respect for homosexuals in word, action and law.

§ 39
- In the *third document* Cardinal Ratzinger instructs Bishops to have legislators approve laws in favor of homosexuals based on human rights but not on homosexuality as such.

§ 40 To close this part of the exposition on conciliar and post-conciliar doctrine on homosexuality, we may say that, in addition to the numerous manifestations of tolerance toward this vice, in none of the documents quoted did the Holy See state that homosexuality is a vice contrary to nature, let alone call to mind that it is one of the sins that cry out to Heaven and clamor to God for vengeance.

§ 41 On analogous doctrine, published on the authority of the U. S. National Conference of Catholic Bishops, the following documents can be consulted: *Principles to Guide Confessors in Questions of Homosexuality* (1973); *To Live in Jesus Christ* (1976); *Called to Compassion and Responsibility* (1989); *Always Our Children* (1997).[46]

3. THE HOMOSEXUAL ISSUE AND THE CATHOLIC CHURCH IN THE UNITED STATES

§ 42 The reason we chose the United States to analyze the situation so far as this issue is concerned is that statistical data are more accessible there, probably due to the great welcome that American public opinion usually gives the publication of statistics. Perhaps people

46. *L'Osservatore Romano*, 7/11/1990, pp. 4f; *Catholic Almanac* (Huntington, Indiana: Our Sunday Visitor, 1999), p. 67.

there talk more about homosexuality and there are more groups of this type of person than in other countries due to the general liberalism that characterized the formation of the United States, as well as to the characteristic of Americans to form associations more readily than other peoples.

Therefore, the overview below is not intended to classify the United States as any more or any less decadent than other countries. We simply take what is happening in the United States as an example of what is happening in the whole world.

Extent of the Phenomenon and Principal Movements

§ 43 A newsletter of the Democratic Party on the 1979 political campaign in the United States (December 13, 1979), according to the book by Fr. Enrique Rueda, *The Homosexual Network,* said, "The gay vote is now so important in national [American] politics . . . that no serious politician can ignore or ridicule it." The document gives the figure of 15 million homosexual Americans of voting age, an estimate confirmed by contributors to the political column of the *Washington Star*.[47]

§ 44 A word should be said about this figure of 15 million. In the beginning of the 1950s, an American biologist, Alfred Kinsey, published the result of a survey of 11,000 people on sex-related subjects. He began with the premise that, in sexual matters, people usually do not tell the truth when interviewed. So he looked for those who voluntarily wished to talk about the subject, which thus included persons primarily in marginal groups. The data collected in this study was in general use until recently. The applications of that study projected an estimated 10 percent of homosexuals in the population,[48] which would mean about 25 million people.

However, in October 1994, a group of three researchers at the University of Chicago and one at New York State University published another study based on 3,500 interviews with selected people carried out by an authoritative public research institute. *Time* magazine con-

47. Enrique Rueda, *The Homosexual Network—Private Lives and Public Policy* (Old Greenwich, CT: Devin Adair Co., 1983), p. 134.
48. Philip Elmer-DeWitt, "Now for the Truth about Americans and Sex," in *Time*, 10/17/1994, pp. 44, 46, 50.

sidered the new study to provide "the first really scientific statistics in America."[49] The researchers contested the Kinsey method as being based on groups deemed atypical. But they also generally recognized, as the weak point of their research, that the sexual topic—especially homosexuality—inhibits people. One of them said: "There is probably much more homosexual activity than what people are saying."[50] They estimated the homosexual population in the United States at 2 percent, or about five million people.

On the basis of this percentage these scholars concluded, among other things, that the danger of AIDS is not so grave as it is trumped up to be and that it needs to be fought only in the so-called high-risk groups. This caused indignation in certain public-health related sectors. The former head of the National Commission on AIDS, for example, commenting on the study, quipped: "The message is shocking and runs against the whole history of the epidemic."[51]

One sees, therefore, that both surveys are controversial. If we want to draw an average between the two—since one claims 25 million and the other five million—we would have the 15 million mentioned by Fr. Rueda in his 1983 book.

But even the more conservative estimate of five million would indicate that homosexuality has become a phenomenon of apocalyptic proportions.

§ 45 Among the principal organizations of homosexuals in the U.S. are the so-called Catholic movements: New Ways Ministry run by a priest and a nun, and Dignity, founded by Jesuit priest John J. McNeill in 1971.[52] Dignity has some 100 chapters in the U.S. and Canada.[53]

Support of the Hierarchy and the Situation of Homosexuality in the American Clergy

§ 46 The first symposium on "Homosexuality and the Catholic Church"

49. *Ibid.*, p. 46.
50. Stuart Michaels, Statement, *ibid.*, p. 48.
51. June Osborn, Statement, *ibid.*, p. 49.
52. E. Rueda, *op. cit.*, pp. 270, 362.
53. *Ibid.*, p. 362.

promoted by New Ways Ministry, whose speakers were all in favor of homosexuality, was held at the Holy Trinity Missionary Seminary at Silver Springs, Maryland, from November 20 to 22, 1981. Twenty-two religious organizations, nearly all Catholic, supported the organization of the event.[54]

§ 47 The National Conference of Catholic Bishops (NCCB) and the United States Catholic Conference (USCC), which comprises the central Church bureaucracy and is the official arm of the NCCB, have supported on various occasions the movement or topic of homosexuality. Fr. Robert Nugent, director of New Ways Ministry and a leader of the homosexual movement, served as a consultant to the USCC. The NCCB's Department of Education published a document entitled "Planning for the Single Young Adult Ministry: Directives for Ministerial Outreach," a work partially written by New Ways Ministry.[55]

§ 48 The efforts of Dignity to influence the NCCB began in 1977. The key figure of the NCCB's Office of Public Affairs and Information became president of Dignity. This movement's relationship with the NCCB gradually grew more intense as time went by. Milestones in this process were: the July 1981 meeting of Dignity's president, Frank Scheuren, with Archbishop John Quinn, Archbishop of San Francisco and President of the NCCB; another meeting with Bishop Thomas Kelly, who held an important post at the Bishops' Conference; Dignity's exchange of correspondence with the next NCCB President, Archbishop John Roach.[56] At the meeting with Archbishop Quinn, according to a Dignity newsletter, "The archbishop has requested that Dignity . . . submit to him proposals that show as to how joint cooperation can be accomplished in the day-to-day pastoral ministry to our people. He expressed that this would be the beginning of an ongoing dialogue between the parties."[57]

§ 49 A booklet published by New Ways Ministry, *Time to Speak*, presented a list of sixteen Bishops, including Cardinal Krol of Philadelphia and Cardinal Dearden of Detroit, who in some way had benefited the homosexual movement.[58] Lending support to the move-

---

54. *Ibid.*, pp. 293ff.
55. *Ibid.*, pp. 306-310.
56. *Ibid.*, pp. 308f.
57. *Ibid.*, pp. 323f.
58. *Ibid.*, p. 316, on which can be found the said list with the date on which each Bishop gave his support.

ment, a letter from Bishop Raymond Hunthausen, then Bishop of Seattle, stands out. It encouraged the efforts of the homosexual movement to make the state's House of Representatives approve a law granting special privileges to homosexuals. A letter from the Archbishop of Milwaukee, Archbishop Rembert Weakland, also spoke favorably about the approval of a law to protect the "basic human rights" of homosexuals.[59] The booklet, *Time to Speak,* also contains a list of 38 Catholic associations that support homosexuals.[60]

§ 50 Dignity has estimated that 75 percent of its meetings are held at Church properties.[61] Some homosexual parties have also taken place on Catholic premises, such as Dignity's ball, a "black and white dress" affair where people of the same sex danced with each other. That ball took place at Rosary Academy in Sparkill, New York on September 12, 1981. Another example was "Cabaret night," held by the same movement in the auditorium of Saint Francis School in New York City on April 7, 1982.[62]

§ 51 How many Catholic priests are homosexual?* The magazine *Newsweek* reports: "In one of the very few studies based on reliable data—1,500 interviews between 1960 and 1985—psychologist Richard Sipe of Maryland, a former priest, concludes that close to 20 percent of the 57,000 Catholic priests in the United States are homosexual and half of them are sexually active. According to Sipe,

59. *Ibid.*, pp. 319f.
60. *Ibid.*, pp. 326f.
61. *Ibid.*, p. 321.
62. *Ibid.*, p. 329.

* *Publisher's Note*: The answer to this question is difficult to determine. Certain estimates have been brought forward, but they must be taken with the proverbial "grain of salt." Although homosexuality obviously exists among priests, we recall the grossly exaggerated "statistics" claimed by abortion advocates in the 1950's and 1960's regarding the number of illegal abortions supposedly being performed at the time. As Dr. Bernard Nathanson, former abortionist, has subsequently admitted, the purpose (and result) of these lies was to spread the idea that "Everyone is doing it anyway, so let's make it legal." It is not impossible that some homosexual advocates are using a similar technique. One should be especially wary of possibly inflated figures coming from anonymous sources, such as "some authorities" and "unofficial sources." We ask the reader to keep these *caveats* in mind when reviewing the estimates that have been offered.

the number of homosexual priests has significantly increased since 1978; other therapists believe the real number today [1987] may be around 40 percent."[63]

§ 52 "The number of priests contaminated with AIDS in the United States grows daily. This disclosure was released in a documentary made by the Conference of Men Religious, an entity that represents 25,000 of the 57,000 American Catholic priests. Non-official estimates put the number of homosexual priests at about 40 percent."[64]

§ 53 *Time* magazine published statements by Fr. Robert Nugent to the effect that "a U. S. survey of vocation directors in men's religious orders showed that, from 1981 to 1985, five percent of candidates accepted for the priesthood identified themselves to the Church as being homosexual in orientation.

"Perhaps the most emotional debates are those now occurring within the Roman Catholic Church. Father Andrew Greeley, the irrepressible U. S. sociologist and novelist, complained in a recent article that regard for priestly celibacy is being undermined by a 'national network' of actively homosexual clergy. 'In some dioceses, certain rectories have become lavender houses,' he grumbled. Theologian Richard McBrien, of the University of Notre Dame, contends that homosexuality is so widespread that 'heterosexual males are deciding in ever larger numbers not even to consider the priesthood.' "[65]

§ 54 "Another clergyman," reports the journalist, "who is a regional director of priestly education in one of the larger men's orders, explained to *Time* the justification for his private homosexual life during recent years. 'We'll never know what is right or wrong until we open up the issue and look at people's experiences,' he said. 'I don't see any contradiction between having an intimate relationship and a total commitment to Christ.' This prominent priest said his superiors have been quietly aware of his long-running, but not live-in, relationship with a fellow gay. They expect him to be judicious, he says, not to change."[66]

---

63. *Newsweek* (New York), "Gays in the Clergy," 2/23/1987.
64. *Folha de S. Paulo*, "AIDS-1," 1/15/1989.
65. Richard Nugent Ostling, "The Battle over Gay Clergy—Demands for Toleration Shake Many North American Churches," in *Time*, 11/13/1989, pp. 44f.
66. *Ibid.*

§ 55 To cite a more recent case, let us look at a story printed in the Catholic newspaper, *The Wanderer* (February 23, 1995):

"Among those entering the ground floor of San Francisco's St. Mary's Cathedral on a Saturday evening, as Mass was being held above, was a tall Asian gentleman wearing a stunning scarlet cocktail dress and long spiked red high heels, arm-in-arm with two shorter men. And as Mass-goers walked out of the cathedral after the 5:30 p.m. Mass, it was hard not to notice affectionate male couples in the cathedral parking lot, hugging and kissing. And a continent and an ocean away, in Vatican offices, fax machines were buzzing as angry San Francisco Catholics informed Rome of the latest sacrilege in their city.

"Two weeks ago, on Feb. 11th, San Francisco's Catholic cathedral was the site for a major celebration of homosexual power in California. The chief political, religious, and social leaders of the homosexual rights movement in the city, state, and nation mingled with their constituents at a fund-raiser for pro-homosexual causes. The scandal and outrage . . . show to what extent the American Church has bought into the homosexual agenda. . . . The event at St. Mary's Cathedral Conference Center was billed as a *Saints Alive* awards celebration and a celebrity auction to benefit the exclusively homosexual Metropolitan Community Church's social service programs. . . . The live auction was conducted by two local gay comedians, whose patter was constant, clever, crass, and peppered with jokes about sodomy. Suzy Berger, an improvisational and stand-up comedienne, ripped off a barrage of smutty homosexual jokes, bathroom humor, asides about 'lesbian culture,' and lurid comments. . . . When a painting, *Study with Fruits and Flowers*, seemed not to be getting many bids, he [the auctioneer] offered to throw in the male model with the deal. The model then turned his backside to the audience, and took a bow. The audience whooped and hollered in excitement. The more outrageous the merchandise, the cruder the MC's were, and the louder the audience. . . . When two one-year scholarships to The Child Unique Montessori School did not receive many bids, the auctioneer offered to throw in one, and then two, sperm donations to lesbians who might like to have a child to use the scholarship."[67]

---

67. *The Wanderer*, "San Francisco Cathedral Is Site For 'Gay Power' Bash," 2/23/1995.

The "McNeill Affair"

§ 56 American (former-) Jesuit John McNeill, who holds a doctorate from the University of Louvain and is the founder of the homosexual movement, Dignity, wrote a book making a theological defense of this vice against nature: *The Church and the Homosexual* (1976).

As far as we know, the work has become an historic milestone on the subject of homosexuality. Aside from the audacity shown by a Catholic priest in publishing a book in defense of this vice, the work can be considered the strongest base for what has since been termed "homosexual theology."

On manifestations of support and criticism that preceded the publishing of his book, McNeill recounts: "After various delays, a final revised copy of the manuscript was sent to Rome in 1975. A reply was finally received in October. In his reply Father Arrupe turned over authority to give 'permission to publish' to the Provincial of the New York Province of the Society of Jesus. He said he would not object to publication granted that certain suggestions and guidelines be accepted and followed."[68]

Soon after Fr. Arrupe made these suggestions, the Congregation for the Doctrine of the Faith published *Declaration on Certain Questions concerning Sexual Ethics*. McNeill communicated to his superiors the interpretation of the *Declaration* he had made in his book. A reply came in a letter (January 28, 1976) from the Jesuit Provincial, Fr. Eamon Taylor, stating: "In my opinion the adjustments you introduced in your manuscript, as we had agreed in a conversation on November 10, respond to the recommendations of the Superior General of September 19 and . . . as a result, I am pleased to be able to grant you the *imprimi potest*, with today's date."[69]

The adjustments suggested by Fr. Arrupe and referred to by Fr. Taylor were probably rather superficial, as McNeill later writes, "I want to assure my readers that at no point was I asked to change or alter my ideas or convictions in any way to be granted official permission for publication."[70]

---

68. J. McNeill, *op. cit.*, pp. xi.
69. Eamon Taylor, Letter responding to Fr. John McNeill, January 28, 1976, *ibid.*
70. *Ibid.*

In November 1986—that is, ten years after the publication of the work—the news broke that Fr. John McNeill had been punished with dismissal from the Society of Jesus on account of his preaching in favor of homosexuality (Marjorie Hyer, "Gay-Rights Priest Faces Expulsion," in *The Washington Post*, 11/8/1986; *Jornal do Brasil*, Rio de Janeiro, 11/9/1986).

On that occasion, the press reported that already in 1977 the Vatican had revoked approval of the book, *The Church and the Homosexual* (M. Hyer, *Ibid.*). That measure was an initiative of Cardinal Franjo Seper, then Prefect of the Congregation for the Doctrine of the Faith, who had also forbidden Fr. McNeill to speak out. After nine years of silence, the General of the Society of Jesus, Fr. Peter Hans Kolvenbach, gave Fr. McNeill the choice of ceasing his homosexual preaching and religious assistance to the movement or of quitting the ranks of the Society of Jesus. McNeill preferred to leave the Jesuit Order rather than give up his ideas (*ibid.*).

The silence previously imposed on McNeill had little practical result, since the public at large was unaware of it; the priest's book continued to be sold widely in English and translated into other languages with the approval of the Jesuit Provincial in New York and the good graces of Fr. Arrupe, then Superior General; for its part, the homosexual movement Dignity, which McNeill founded, has not been hindered in its expansion.

Undoubtedly, the punishment of 1986 that dismissed the priest from the Society of Jesus was a moral and disciplinary sanction. But, from another standpoint, it was also a political disengagement from McNeill's ideas on the part of the Order. Now the priest is free to continue his work and to speak at will without compromising the Society. No word ever came out in the press about any threats by the Holy See to pronounce McNeill a heretic or excommunicate him, thus hindering his freedom of movement and expression outside the Order. On the contrary, the record shows only the surprising benevolence of New York Jesuit Provincial, Fr. David Tolan, who calls McNeill "an extraordinarily good man" who "tried to stick to the letter of the law established for him" (*Ibid.*).

Fr. Tolan added that McNeill continues to be a priest whose situation, to be regularized, needs only for a Bishop to accept him in his diocese.

Therefore, taking into account Fr. Tolan's benevolence, one should ask whether at least several heavyweight Jesuits did not, in effect, grant McNeill the freedom to continue his preaching without compromising the Society of Jesus.

The Society of Jesus adopted a similar political procedure in relation to Fr. Hans Urs von Balthasar, who in 1950 was also released from

In addition to denying Catholic doctrine on homosexuality, McNeill contends that this vice should play a social role of equilibrium between a masculine culture and feminist demands.[71] In this sense, he makes his own a comment by Jung on the social "mission" of homosexuals: "This [homosexuality] gives a great capacity for friendship, which creates bonds of admirable tenderness between men and can even rescue friendship between sexes from the limbo of the impossible. An individual can have a good taste and aesthetic sensibility nourished by the presence of a feminine vein. . . . He often possesses a great wealth of religious sentiments, which helps lead him to practice the *ecclesia spiritualis*."[72]

Homosexuality allegedly also has a great role to play in the quest for peace, since, lacking the decisive and combative characteristics of a man, homosexuals could more easily control violence. Furthermore, because of his "sweetness," the homosexual is very inclined to serve others, and his "femininity" leads him to make a contribution to humanity in the appreciation of aesthetic and religious values.[73] As he describes the role of the homosexual in the religious ambit, McNeill points to Our Lord Jesus Christ as model.[74]

Jesuit obedience to be able to devote himself more fully to the foundation of his Secular Institute, the *Johannesgemeinschaft*. At the time a pioneering and audacious initiative, the institute is viewed today as one of the probable blueprints for the Church of the future. Von Balthasar himself explains: "The split of which I had a premonition took place in fact when I faced my duty to obey a formal order of Saint Ignatius, to abandon—much to my displeasure—my spiritual motherland, the Society of Jesus, in order to achieve a kind of prolongation of his idea in the world" (Hans Urs von Balthasar, "Von Balthasar: la mia opera è abbozzata più che terminata," in *L'Osservatore Romano*, 6/24/1984, p. 4).

Are they not using the same procedure with McNeill?

71. J. McNeill, *op. cit.*, pp. 132, 138-139.
72. Carl Gustav Jung, *The Collected Works* (New York: Pantheon, 1959), vol. IX, P. I, pp. 86f., in *ibid.*, pp. 194f.
73. J. McNeill, *op. cit.*, pp. 130-135.
74. *Ibid.*, pp. 208f.

The Chicago Symposium

§ 57 The scandal of homosexuality in the Church took on hitherto unheard-of proportions when homosexuals assembled in Chicago on March 27-29, 1992, with the support and presence of some Bishops.

The symposium was sponsored by 91 diocesan offices and religious communities. About 39 percent of the participants held leadership posts in religious orders, parishes and other institutions; 63 percent were priests, nuns and religious.[75]

The *Catholic News Service* distributed a press communique on the meeting entitled "Bishops Urge Less Rigid Church Attitude toward Homosexuals." It reads: "Three Catholic bishops speaking at a forum on 'Lesbian and Gay People and Catholicism' said that they hoped pastoral leaders would adopt less rigid attitudes toward homosexual men and women. On March 26, Bishop Kenneth E. Untener of Saginaw, Michigan, Bishop William A. Hughes of Covington, Kentucky, and auxiliary Bishop Thomas J. Gumbleton of Detroit addressed a symposium in Chicago, organized by New Ways Ministry. The organization . . . seeks understanding for and acceptance of gays and lesbians in the Catholic community. Bishop Hughes, who chaired the U. S. Bishops' task force that drafted 'The Many Faces of AIDS: A Gospel Response,' said that . . . Christians are called to be a people of compassion, aware of the difficulties and the struggles people face. He likened the church's changing pastoral approach to gays and lesbians to its experience in embracing divorcees and survivors of suicide. He said that such an outreach obviously did not endorse divorce or suicide."[76]

---

75. Robert McClory, "Bishops Buck Criticism, Attend Gay Symposium in Chicago," in *The National Catholic Reporter,* 4/10/1992.
76. Keith Picher, "Bishops Urge Less Rigid Church Attitude toward Homosexuals," in *Catholic News Service,* 3/31/1992.

    This news release, of which we left out several paragraphs, was published by the Archdiocese of Chicago newspaper *The New World*, on 4/3/1992 and by innumerable other papers in the U.S. such as *The Long Island Catholic*, 4/1/1992; *Mississippi Today*, Jackson, 4/3/1992; *The Messenger*, Belleville, 4/3/1992; *The Catholic Free Press*, Worcester, 4/3/1992; *The Catholic Review*, Baltimore, 4/8/1992; *Catholic Herald*, Milwaukee, 4/9/1992; *Catholic Courier*, Rochester, 4/9/1992; *The*

In a comprehensive report for *The Wanderer*, Eric Bower adds other important details:

> Bishop Gumbleton was enthusiastically applauded by the 500 plus participants when he said: "I am proud to be here! Pleased to be here! And honored to be with you!" He continued: "Be patient and ready to wait until the Bishops and priests show compassion, love and care for all those in the gay community."
>
> Outside the main conference room, various display tables were set up featuring literature, tapes and other information on homosexuality. A display table sponsored by Dignity also offered literature advertising the services of AGLO (Joseph Cardinal Bernardin's personally supervised Archdiocesan Gay and Lesbian Organization). The same table offered pornographic homosexual literature.
>
> Bishop William Hughes of Covington celebrated a strange "mass" for the meeting's participants in the ballroom of the Westin Hotel. Coffee was served before it began. The makeshift sanctuary consisted of a platform with a stack chair and a small table on it. On the table was a punch bowl. No crucifix. The wine for the "mass" was a gallon of Gallo served in chalices. The bread was coarse and falling in crumbs. Participants served themselves unceremoniously. After the "mass," wine cups, plates and napkins were left in the ballroom.[77]

Richard Freeman, president of the Catholic Action League, described the conference as "perhaps the most blatant and dramatic example we have yet seen of how far gone some of our Bishops are and how little discipline is being exercised by the Vatican. . . . Our

---

Monitor, Trenton, 4/9/1992; *The Message*, Evansville, 4/10/1992; *The Catholic Sentinel*, Portland, 4/10/1992; *Catholic Telegraph*, Cincinnati, 4/10/1992; *The Florida Catholic*, Miami, 4/10/1992; *New Catholic Explorer*, Joliet, 4/10/1992; *Catholic East Texas*, Tyler, 4/10/1992; *The Green Bay Catholic Compass*, 4/10/1992; *The Catholic Post*, Peoria, 4/12/1992; *Northwest Indiana Catholic,* 4/12/1992; *The Catholic Virginian*, Richmond, 4/13/1992; *The Catholic Messenger*, Davenport, 4/16/1992; *Twin Circle*, 4/19/1992; *The Providence Visitor*, Rhode Island, 4/23/1992; *The Saint Cloud Visitor*, 4/23/1992; *Acadiana Catholic*, Lafayette, May 1992; *Inland Catholic*, San Bernardino & Riverside Counties, May 1992.

77. Eric Bower, "Give Lip Service to Rome, Encourage Dissident Homosexuals," in *The Wanderer*, 4/9/1992.

renegade Bishops and Cardinal seem to fear nothing and no one, least of all God. We are moving very, very close to a formal break with Rome and a complete disintegration of the structure of the Church in this nation."[78]

Freeman said that it was no accident that Chicago was picked for the site of the conference. Under Cardinal Bernardin, he observed, it had become notorious for its inner-Church homosexual activism. According to a well-informed source, Cardinal Bernardin was invited to address the conference. However, perhaps because he was embroiled in a priestly pedophilia scandal,[79] he declined the invitation. But he gave it his formal blessing and singled out his three brother Bishops who attended the conference for special praise.[80]

Homosexuals' "Religious Orders"

§ 58 Special mention should be made of a little publicized phenomenon, the foundation of so-called religious orders exclusively for

---

78. See also news item in *The Eternal Call*, Park Forest, Ill, Pentecost 1992.
79. Accused of sexually molesting a seminarian in 1975 (*Veja*, "Processado," 11/17/1993), an event that had worldwide repercussions (*Corriere della Sera*, "Ricevuto dal Papa cardinale accusato di abusi sessuali," 1/5/1994), Cardinal Joseph Bernardin was acquitted for lack of evidence (Kenneth L. Woodward, "Was It Real or Memories?" in *Newsweek*, 3/14/1994).
80. a. The Vatican's reaction to these events in North America was one of extreme moderation. In July 1992, the Congregation for the Doctrine of the Faith released the document it had sent to the U.S. Bishops justifying, as we have seen, certain limitations to the civil rights of homosexuals and reaffirming principles already issued on the matter in the letter the same Congregation had sent the world Episcopate in 1986 on the subject (Congregation for the Doctrine of the Faith, "Alcune considerazioni concernenti la risposta a proposte di legge sulla non-discriminazione delle persone omosessuali," 2nd version, July 23, 1992, in *L'Osservatore Romano*, 7/24/1992).

    The "Considerazioni" were published with a few alterations (*Ibid.*), along with comments by Vatican spokesman Navarro-Valls. He said that the document "was not intended as a public and official instruction . . . but to help those who have to evaluate projected bills on the

Catholic homosexuals. Such "orders," described in *The Homosexual Network,* still had not been recognized by the Church authorities near

---

matter" (Joaquim Navarro-Valls, Statements to the press, in *Avvenire*, "Chiarezza, non discriminazione," 7/24/1992; "Responding to Legislative Proposals on Discriminations against Homosexuals," in *Origins—CNS Documentary Service*, 8/6/1992, pp. 173-177).

The reaction of American Bishops to this Vatican document can be gauged by this article of the *San Francisco Chronicle* entitled: "S.F. Archdiocese Opposes Vatican Letter on Gay Bias Law." It reads: "Local Roman Catholic church leaders said yesterday that they will continue to oppose laws that discriminate against homosexuals—despite a Vatican missive declaring that gays and lesbians do not have the same civil rights as heterosexuals" (Don Lattin, in *San Francisco Chronicle*, 7/25/1992).

The article goes on to say that the Holy See document "contradicts past statements by San Francisco Archbishop John Quinn. . . . Quinn was on vacation yesterday . . . but the Rev. Robert McElroy, the archbishop's representative on the archdiocese's Justice and Peace Commission, said, 'There is no change in the archdiocese's policy.' . . . But aides to several of the bishops said they doubt the Vatican document will lead to any change in their tolerance policies toward gays. 'Most of the bishops would rather just ignore this,' said one priest, a seasoned observer of the American bishops' conference" (*Ibid.*).

Archbishop Rembert G. Weakland of Milwaukee, a prominent leader of the Church's liberal wing, "noted that the statement carried no signature and that there was no indication that it had been seen by the Pope" (Peter Steinfels, "Vatican Condones Gay-Rights Limits," in *The New York Times*, 7/18/1992).

b. Practical measures opposed to the Holy See's guidelines were not long in coming. As a matter of fact, a symptomatic example is the work carried out by Archbishop John Roach and the Minnesota Catholic Conference (MCC) supporting the law barring discrimination against homosexuals in employment, housing, education and public accommodations in that state. Not only did the MCC support passage of the bill, it helped to author the bill. MCC executive director Msgr. James Habiger urged approval of the bill in these words: "The Catholic Church recognizes and affirms the human dignity and worth of gay persons and calls for the protection of their basic human rights" (James Habiger, Argumentation in support of the law preventing discrimination against homosexuals, in Paul Likoudis, "Minnesota Catholic Conference Helps Write and Pass Homosexual Rights Bill," in *The Wanderer,* 4/1/1993).

the end of 1982 when it was published. Some of the main groups include the following:

§ 59 Agape Community—a religious extension of Dignity: Its members may, if they so desire, make promises of poverty, chastity and obedience. "Lovers," says the rule, "are welcome together or without their partners. . . . While ideally chastity or love commitments are to be encouraged, the community is open to all who seek to be witnesses to Christ."[81]

§ 60 Emmaus House, formerly called St. Matthew Community: Its rule says it is an entity made up primarily of Catholic homosexuals who serve the Church in a variety of ministries. Any member who wishes may make private vows of celibacy, obedience and poverty under the orientation of the spiritual director and the approval of the Diocesan Bishop.[82]

§ 61 Christian Community Association: It has several degrees of spirituality, of which the most advanced requires a monastic lifestyle. Vows of poverty, obedience and chastity were re-baptized with the names sharing, commitment and charity. A postulant must recite this formula: "I believe that homosexuality is a gift from God and that we have an obligation to use our gifts in the service of humanity and that this is one way in which we return our gift to God, through religious community."[83]

§ 62 Other similar organizations: Augustinians of Charity, The Order of Transformation, and the Morning Star Community.[84]

4. THE VICE OF PEDOPHILIA

§ 63 The problem of pedophilia, this moral aberration of cowardice, cruelty and homosexuality, has been causing devastation in ecclesiastical circles. News items in magazines and papers portray a rising tide of scandal caused by priests who abuse children.

Some widely publicized facts permit us to gauge how deeply this

---

81. E. Rueda, *op. cit.*, p. 350.
82. *Ibid.*, pp. 351, 581.
83. *Ibid.*, p. 352.
84. *Ibid.*, pp. 351ff.
85. "Padre americano será julgado por tara sexual," *Zero Hora* (Porto Alegre, Brazil), 10/14/1985.

moral wound has affected more than just a few ecclesiastics. It appears as another serious consequence of the liberal customs that have installed themselves in the clergy largely due to the conciliar reforms.

§ 64 A terrible scandal broke out in the United States in 1985 when Fr. Gilbert Gauthe, of the Diocese of Lafayette, Louisiana, confessed to having sexually abused 37 boys. He was accused of 23 counts of rape, pornography and crimes against nature.[85]

§ 65 Cases of sexual abuse of children—which justly caused indignation in Catholic public opinion—tripled in a short time. The next year, 1986, a contributor to *The National Catholic Reporter* (NCR), wrote: "Since the NCR report on pedophilia cases involving Catholic priests a year ago, the number of priests accused, indicted or convicted of sexual misconduct with adolescents has more than tripled. Fr. Thomas Doyle, a Dominican who worked at the Apostolic Nunciature in Washington, speaking at a meeting of canonists in Morristown, New Jersey early this month, figured that [from 1985 to 1986] there were from 40 to 50 cases in the U.S. 'This is the most serious problem the Church has faced in the last few centuries,'"[86] he said.

Another contributor to the same paper comments: "The incendiary and painful experience [of the Diocese] of Lafayette [where Fr. Gauthe's affair took place] was a mere lightning launching a disquieting, and at times sinister light, on the problem of child abuse in the Catholic Church as a whole in the United States, and that findings on a national scale can be devastating. Many dioceses are no longer able to obtain insurance covering sexual infractions of the clergy, and some sources indicate that penal lawsuits for sexual abuse may cost the Church one billion dollars in the next ten years—especially if preventive and corrective measures are not taken."[87]

§ 66 In 1989 the United States Catholic Conference assembled for one week in Baltimore. One of the topics studied was the "pedophilia of some priests and bishops."

This topic of pedophilia, a journalist says, "is the most worrisome

---

86. Thomas Doyle, Statements on pedophilia in the USA, in Jason Berry, "Dioceses React to Deepening Dilemma," in *The National Catholic Reporter*, 5/30/1986.
87. Tim McCarthy, "Church Still on Trial in Pedophilia Crisis," *ibid.*

subject. After all, 300 cases of priests who have sexually molested minors have been reported to the authorities, and the Church has had to cough up 50 million dollars in settlements with the victims in order to avoid greater scandal. . . . Right at the opening of the meeting, the Catholic movement Open Church founded in Washington accused one of the Bishops present of having engaged in sexual relations with a thirteen-year-old boy seven years earlier. The victim's mother . . . appeared at a press interview to confirm the accusation. A second denunciation was made by a student just over 20 years of age, who disclosed that when in high school he had had sexual relations with a priest (who is now a Bishop), who paid him for it. The young man also claimed that the priest paid for several trips so they could meet in some other town. The Bishops counter-attacked with a communique saying that these denunciations had already been examined by the Pope's own representative in the United States, Archbishop Pio Laghi, and that no solid evidence had been found."[88]

§ 67 In 1992 the number of churchmen accused of pedophilia rose to 400, and Church legal expenditures reached $400 million.[89]

Such figures keep rising. A writer in *Newsweek* notes this about child molestation by priests: "While allegations have been lodged against an estimated 400 priests since 1982, some churchmen extrapolate* that as many as 2,500 priests have molested children or teenagers."[90]

Some people claim such figures are even higher: "Precise data are lacking, but the author of a book entitled *Lead Us Not into Temptation* estimated that from 1983 to this day, 400 priests have been sued in penal or civil courts. Richard Sipe, who left the priesthood and works as a psychotherapist at Johns Hopkins School of Medicine, calculated that 6 percent [that is, 3,180] of the 53,000 American priests have had sexual contacts with minors. He figured that over the last few years the Church has paid between 200 to 500 mil-

---

88. José Meirelles Passos, "Acusações de sexo e racismo envolvem Bispos americanos," in *O Globo*, 11/7/1989.
89. Data taken from the book of Jason Berry entitled *Lead Us Not into Temptation* (New York: Doubleday, 1992), in K. L. Woodward, "The Sins of the Fathers," in *Newsweek*, 6/1/1992, p. 57; Jemez Springs, "Sins of the Fathers," in *The Economist*, 6/18/1992, p. 50.

* See *Publisher's Note*, p. 30 above.

90. Aric Press, "Priests and Abuse," in *Newsweek*, 8/16/1993, p. 40.

lion dollars in legal fees and compensation to families. The price of silence."[91]

Another source confirms this and adds more details: "According to a survey recently published in the American press, cases of sexual molestation occurring in American parishes over the last 20 years reportedly involve from 2,000 to 4,000 priests and about 100,000 victims, mostly women and children."[92]

A more recent publication estimates that Church expenditures for victim compensation in the U.S. have reached $650 million.[93]

§ 68 In **Canada**, Fr. Denis Vadeboncoeur, pastor of St. Benedict Parish in Sainte-Foy, was accused of molesting four adolescents on counts of gross indecency, sexual aggression and sodomy. The priest admitted his guilt.[94]

Sectors of public opinion in **Brazil** were indignant and dismayed over the scandal of Brazilian priest Frederico Cunha, found guilty of homosexuality and accused of homicide in the Island of Madeira, **Portugal**. After trying to seduce a 15-year-old boy, he threw the boy off a cliff, killing him. The priest is said to have set up a false alibi. He alleged that at the time of the crime, he was with another 19-year-old adolescent, his godson and a homosexual partner. He was condemned to 12 years in prison for homicide and another 18 months for a homosexual attempt on a minor.[95]

---

91. Rodolfo Brancoli, "Linea verde contro preti pedofili," in *Corriere della Sera*, 9/24/1992; cf. Randall Samborn, "Priest Playing Hardball to Battle Abuse Charges," in *The National Law Journal*, July 1994.
92. Orazio la Rocca, "Wojtyla: 'Piango I preti tentati dai vizi del sesso,'" in *La Repubblica*, 12/22/1993; *Corriere della Sera*, "Molestie, mea culpa dei vescovi," 11/18/1994.
93. Alessio Alticheri, "In Irlanda la Chiesa si scusa per pedofilia," in *Corriere della Sera*, 10/10/1995.
94. Louise Lemiex, "Selon un psychiatre—le père Vadeboncoeur victime d'un 'dérapage' émotionnel," in *Le Soleil* (Quebec), 8/23/1985.
95. Cristina Duran, "Padre brasileiro é condenado em Portugal," in *O Estado de S. Paulo*, 3/11/1993; "Padre brasileiro deve recorrer da sentença," in *O Estado de S. Paulo*, 3/22/1993; Mario Prata, "Senhor Cunha ou Fred do caniçal?," *ibid.*; "Pecados na sacristia," *Veja*, 3/17/1993, p. 83.

§ 69 The April 1995 *Adista* bulletin carries this news on the Spanish Catholic hierarchy: "**Spain** is now treading the same path taken in the United States: The scourge of sexual molestation by members of the clergy appears to be spreading like an oil slick. Two cardinals and five bishops are said to be guilty of concealing a network for corrupting minors which involves priests. There are reports of rapes and the sexual abuse of women and psychopaths. The accusation was made by writer and journalist Pepe Rodriguez, who wrote a book on the topic entitled *La vida sexual del clero*. . . . The accusation, which was made as the book was launched on March 7 . . . reports first and last names: Narcis Jubany, Cardinal Emeritus of Barcelona, Cardinal Ricardo Maria Carles, the present Archbishop of Barcelona, with his three auxiliary Bishops, Msgr. Carlos Soler, Msgr. Jaime Traserra and Msgr. Juan-Enric Vives, stand accused of supporting the network. But it does not stop here: Rodriguez also made accusations against the Bishop of Cartagena, Msgr. Javier Azagra . . . and denounced the Bishop of Cuenca, Msgr. José Guerra Campos, for covering up cases of sexual abuse perpetrated by a priest who was guilty, among other things, of raping a mentally handicapped person."[96]

§ 70 In **Austria,** the "Gröer affair" was a highly publicized scandal. Here is a brief overview:

On March 26, 1995, *Profil,* a Viennese weekly with a circulation of 100,000, published the accusations of agronomic engineer Josef Hartmann, a former seminarian who had been in Hollabrunn during the time Hans Hermann Gröer was a professor there. Hartmann accused Cardinal Gröer of the crime of pedophilia between 1972 and 1976.[97] The text of the interview was said to have been sent to Cardinal Gröer three days before it was published. The Cardinal reportedly failed to answer.[98]

---

96. "In Spagna due cardinale e cinque vescovi accusati di silenzio sugli abusi di minori e psicolabili," *Adista*, 4/1/1995.
97. "Ero seminarista, l'arcivescovo abusò di me," *Corriere della Sera*, 3/27/1995.
98. Francesco Strazzari, "Di caso in caso," in *Il Regno*, Bologna, May 1995, p. 264.

By April 3, the number of ex-alumni who were accusing the Cardinal of pedophilia had risen to nine. A Benedictine priest, Fr. Udo Fischer, said that in 1971 Cardinal Gröer had tried to seduce him, a fact that he had reported to the competent authorities in 1985. Nonetheless, eleven months later, Gröer was designated Archbishop of Vienna.[99] In April of 1995, another newspaper, *Bild,* narrated—with details that lacked all decorum and decency—the accusations of five witnesses against the Cardinal.[100] On April 5, 1995, Cardinal Gröer was re-elected to the presidency of the Austrian Bishops' Conference. One day later, he resigned the post. A public opinion poll showed that 62 percent of Austrians believed the Cardinal should relinquish all official duties,[101] and a growing number of personages suggested that he retire.[102]

On April 13, the Vatican named Bishop Christoph von Schönborn as *coadjutor*, or assistant with the right to succeed Cardinal Gröer.[103]

On April 22, the news broke that several women were also accusing the Cardinal of Vienna of having molested them as children. The women claimed that he had taken them to his home on the pretext of giving spiritual direction. Theologian Adolph Holl told *Der Spiegel* that the news caused no surprise among the churchmen of Vienna, who were already aware of "Gröer's weakness for adolescents." A public opinion survey showed that 81 percent of Austrians wanted Cardinal Gröer to be removed from office.[104]

§ 71 On August 1, 1995 a journalist of the *Corriere della Sera* published an article reporting that a spokesman for the Austrian homosexual movement Hosi, Kurt Krickler, said that one-fourth of all the members of the country's Bishops' Conference practiced the sin of Sodom and Gomorrha. One of the accused was Msgr. Christoph von Schön-

---

99. Vivianne Schnitzer, "Más denuncias de homosexualidad contra el cardenal Gröer," in *El País*, 4/3/1995.
100. "Neuen Zeugen im Sex-Skandal," *Bild*, 4/5/1995.
101. "Vienna, il cardinale cede," *Corriere della Sera*, 4/7/1995.
102. F. Strazzari, *op. cit.*, p. 265.
103. Celso Itiberê, "Escândalos sexuais que envolvem padres põem Vaticano na defensiva," in *O Globo*, 4/14/1995; R. N. Ostling, "An Unholy Holy Week," in *Time*, 4/24/1995.
104. Alfredo Venturi, "Vienna ora ripudia il Cardinale Gröer," in *Corriere della Sera*, 4/22/1995.

born, whom the Pope had called to replace Cardinal Gröer when he was accused of pedophilia. "I hope to disclose it tomorrow," said Krickler. "In a press conference we will announce five names, but I still don't know which ones. The list is very long. We will publish names picked at random at the last moment."[105]

§ 72 Referring to the suit against Joseph Louis Cardinal Bernardin of Chicago, who was absolved because his accuser recanted, the homosexual spokesman contended: "We are not satisfied with gossip-mongers. We have carefully gathered documentation and information from various sources. We are very sure of what we are saying." The reason alleged for such denunciations is to make Austrian law more tolerant of homosexuals. Although the law permits persons over 16 to have homosexual and lesbian relationships, male homosexuals believe they are being discriminated against. They take as a model an Italian law that establishes age 14 as the threshold age for any kind of sexual relationship.[106]

In fact, the next day Krickler fulfilled his promise and disclosed the names of five Bishops whom he claimed were homosexuals. Heading the list was Msgr. Christoph von Schönborn, auxiliary Bishop of Vienna with right of succession, followed by Msgr. Egon Kapelari, Bishop of Klagenfurt; Msgr. Andreas Laun, Bishop of Salzburg; Msgr. Klaus Küng, titular Bishop of the Diocese of Feldkirch, and finally, the now deceased Msgr. Leopold Ungar. Krickler claimed that he could produce three witnesses to testify against each of the Bishops, but he failed to present them. The four Prelates stated that the accusations were groundless and announced legal proceedings against Krickler.[107]

§ 73 At the beginning of July, the news broke that a petition drive with progressivist tones had gathered as many as 400,000 signatures from among the Austrian population. The cause for this general indignation was the "Gröer scandal." And while the Cardinal was known to

---

105. Kurt Krickler, Statement, in Riccardo Chiaberne, "Vienna, ricatto gay alla Chiesa," in *Corriere della Sera*, 8/1/1995.
106. *Ibid.*
107. Alfredo Venturi, "Austria, vescovi alla gogna," in *Corriere della Sera*, 8/2/1995; *La Vanguardia*, Barcelona, "Un líder gay afirma que quatro obispos austriacos son homosexuales," 8/2/1995; *ABC*, "El Papa acepta la renuncia del Cardinal austriaco Gröer, que se retira a un convento," 8/16/1995.

adhere to a Church policy called "conservative," some of the requests in the petition included the abolition of priestly celibacy, the ordination of women and the possibility to veto Vatican choices for Bishops via a plebiscite.[108] The "definitive result" of the petition was published a few days later: 505,000 signatures, including those of 1,000 Austrian priests.[109]

Such is the overview of the "Gröer affair." By April of 1995, Cardinal Gröer had already resigned his post as president of the Austrian Bishops' Conference. However, only in August 1995 was he notified that the Vatican would accept his resignation; it would be effective September 14.[110]

§ 74 In **Ireland**, Cardinal Primate Cohal Daly went public to "present the humble apologies" of the Catholic Church for the long series of sexual molestation of boys by priests that had recently surfaced. Daly admitted that "these terrible violations of sacred trust" had caused "huge wounds in many boys and in their families." After a three-day meeting with the 34 Catholic Bishops of Ireland, he promised that from now on new cases would be transferred to the police, as required by law.

One journalist commented, "This is the most authoritative admission of the drama now undermining the confidence of the faithful in the Catholic Church, the historic mainstay of Irish society. . . . According to the bishops, 1.5 percent of the clergy have been investigated for sexual abuse; sixty priests are alleged to be involved (the number rises to 100 if priests from religious orders are included). However, the question is not one of statistics but of morals. And it is even a question of politics if one takes into account the resignation of Prime Minister Albert Reynolds, who helped bring about the cease-fire in Ulster. Reynolds is said to have prevented the extradition to Ulster of a priest, Brendan Smyth, accused of molesting a young man."[111]

---

108. Vivianne Schnitzer, "Amenaza de cisma en la Iglesia Católica austriaca tras el 'caso Gröer,' " in *El País*, 7/4/1995.
109. Tito Sansa, " 'Rivoluzione in Chiesa'—Referendum choc tra gli austriaci," in *La Stampa*, Turin, 7/6/1995.
110. *ABC*, *Ibid*.
111. A. Alticheri, "In Irlanda la Chiesa si scusa per pedofilia," in *Corriere della Sera*, 10/13/1995.

5. ECCLESIASTICAL HOMOSEXUALITY IN OTHER COUNTRIES

§ 75 In **Brazil**, a journalist of *O Estado de S. Paulo* revealed in two reports and an interview that 15 priests had died of AIDS in the São Paulo metropolitan area from 1988 to 1993.[112] Rumor has it that the actual figure is even higher.

§ 76 To us, it seemed very significant that the Gay Group of Bahia awarded the Cardinal-Archbishop of São Paulo, Msgr. Paulo Evaristo Arns, the "rose triangle trophy" in recognition of his defense of homosexuals' rights.[113]

§ 77 Father Jacques Perotti provides some data that allows one to gauge the degree that the vice of homosexuality has been accepted in the clergy of **France**. The private secretary of the well-known Abbé Pierre says: "I am a priest and a homosexual, and I belong to a French organization called David and Jonathan which has existed for 21 years and which brings together homosexual men and women. . . . It is a lay movement. Priests and women religious also take part in it. . . . In the United States some studies were carried out, and they believe that between 20 and 30 percent of the priests are homosexuals. It must be similar in all countries of the world."[114]

Describing how he came to terms with his homosexuality, Perotti tells how he stopped exercising his priestly functions and was later given support to resume them: "I lived outside the Church from 1969 to 1981, working on different things just like anyone else. It was during this time that I discovered the homosexual world with its miseries, its sufferings and its hopes. Then, in 1981, I returned to see my Bishop and told him: 'I return bearing in me a world I will never leave, the world of my homosexual brothers.' And he accepted me. Since I did not want to return to a parish, for that would prevent me

---

112. Roldão Arruda, "A Aids chega à Igreja," in *O Estado de S. Paulo*, 10/22/1993; "D. Angélico nega que Igreja esconda doentes," in *O Estado de S. Paulo*, 10/23/1993; "A Igreja Católica se destaca no apoio aos doentes de Aids," in *O Estado de S. Paulo*, 10/24/1993.
113. "Grupo gay da Bahia dá troféu a D. Paulo," *O Estado de S. Paulo*, 5/25/1995.
114. Jacques Perotti, "Todo amor es sagrado," interview with Maria Urruzola, in *El País* (Montevideo), 3/4/1994.

from appearing publicly as a homosexual, and since I had known Abbé Pierre since 1954, it occurred to me that I might be able to work with him. . . . In 1981, I went to see him. Abbé Pierre spoke with my Bishop, and ever since I have been on a mission with Abbé Pierre, to minister to him. It is a priestly mission, but I am allowed freedom of expression."[115]

Newsweek magazine adds: "Gays and the Church build bridges also in France. Jacques Perotti, a priest who left the Church when he realized it was impossible to reconcile his homosexuality with his [religious] vocation, helped found a group known as David and Jonathan, which maintains study groups, prayer meetings and debates on the moral dilemmas faced by gays. Though the organization, with 30 centers around France and 1,500 members, is not a group officially recognized by the Church, it has frequent contacts with Catholic bishops, and at times the Church lends its premises for their meetings."[116]

§ 78 As far as the "Gaillot affair" is concerned, *The Catholic Herald* of London published in passing this bit of news: "In the mid-eighties, [Msgr. Gaillot] admitted that he was an homosexual."[117]

§ 79 A survey in **Holland** would indicate that a large number of parish priests in that country have turned away from the teaching of the Magisterium of the Church on homosexuality.

Fr. van der Ploeg writes: "In a local paper dated April 15 of last year, we found a communique entitled 'Parish Priests Reject Church Doctrine on Homosexuality.' The Union of Pastoral Agents carried out a survey among 757 pastors of the archdiocese of Utrecht to find out their opinion about 'homosexual conduct of parish priests.' Only 350 of the 750 pastors responded to the survey. Experts consider this to be a high percentage, which they deem representative of the whole. However, it should be noted that a certain number of priests may not have responded because they viewed the survey as abusive to their privacy.

"Of the 350 parish priests who answered the survey, 86 percent (that is, 301) are at odds with the Church position on homosexuality. As a consequence, these gentlemen place themselves outside the

115. *Ibid.*
116. "Gays in the Clergy," *Newsweek*, 2/23/1987.
117. "John Paul Meets with Gaillot," *The Catholic Herald*, London, 3/10/1995.

Church. A beautiful archdiocese, where 301 parish priests view the sin of Sodom and Gomorrha as licit and want to bring it inside the Church! Furthermore, 84 percent of the 350 (i.e., 294), believe that 'men who regularly practice homosexual relations' and who are not obliged to celibacy, may be designated pastors. And this is not in Sodom and Gomorrha, but in the archdiocese of Utrecht! How can one trust a 'parish priest' in the archdiocese of Utrecht? In Holland, the Church has become a Church in exile."[118]

A more recent survey says: "In Holland, where an open and vigorous debate has long been taking place about some of the most basic principles of Catholic doctrine, a coalition of 90 men religious formed the Work Group of Catholic Homosexual Priests. Group members have met with a delegation of bishops to discuss the gay clergy issue. Evidently, meetings have produced no substantial change in Church procedures. But the group was encouraged by the recent survey it conducted among 375 priests of the archdiocese of Utrecht: 84 percent said they had a positive opinion of homosexuality and 28 percent admitted to being homosexuals."[119]

§ 80 Telltale of the situation of some of the clergy in **Spain** are the blasphemous and arrogant statements by Fr. Emili Boils. At the IX Congress of Theology held in Madrid in September 1989, he said: "I am homosexual by nature and by the grace of God, as a believer and a religious. . . . I am neither 'corrupt' nor 'scum' nor a shameful [son] of darkness,' nor is my sin 'nefarious,' nor does my abnormality 'cry out to heaven,' nor am I 'sick' or 'abominable.' . . . I am not a Sodomite. I was not born in such an exotic place [Sodom], nor was I born more than twenty centuries ago. . . . Enough of this crap! . . . I am a priest because I am homosexual."[120]

§ 81 As far as **England** is concerned, we will delve only into the "Hume affair," which caused scandal in March and April of 1995. The case

118. J. van der Ploeg, Survey among Utrecht parish priests, in *Katholieke Stemmen* (Tiburg), June-July 1983, pp. 275f.
119. "Gays in the Clergy," *Newsweek*, 2/23/1987.
120. Emili Boils, "Declaraciones en el IX Congreso de Teología—Iglesia y derechos humanos, Evangelio y liberación," Madrid, 1990, in *Covadonga-Informa* (Madrid), May 1990, p. 8.

had two aspects: the doctrinal and the political-ecclesiastical.

From the *doctrinal standpoint,* **Cardinal Basil Hume**, Archbishop of Westminster and Cardinal Primate of England and Wales, released a statement to the press about homosexuality.[121] On some points, it goes even beyond the concessions to homosexuality made in the documents of the Holy See and clashes with Catholic tradition. It says: "The Church recognizes the dignity of all people and does not define or label them in terms of their sexual orientation."[122] Further on: "The particular orientation or inclination of the homosexual person is not a moral failing. . . . Being a homosexual person is, then, neither morally good nor morally bad; it is homosexual genital acts that are morally wrong."[123]

On issuing this statement, the Cardinal is guilty of equivocation on some points.

§ 82 *First*, by reducing moral culpability only to acts, Msgr. Hume appears to legitimize sinful thoughts and words, which can cause equal culpability in concessions to the vice of homosexuality or to any other vice, as Catholic doctrine has always taught. Thus, this omission by the Cardinal can hardly sit well with Church teaching.

§ 83 *Second,* by reducing the moral culpability of homosexuals to genital acts, Cardinal Hume appears to legitimize a series of libidinous acts between these people that can range from necking, hugging and kissing, to acts more directly offensive to morals such as manual or oral contact with private parts, which nonetheless are not explicitly "genital acts." The Primate of England also appears to legitimize a series of unnatural practices common to a certain type of homosex-

---

121. Basil Hume, "A Note on the Teaching of the Catholic Church concerning Homosexual People," in *Briefing* (London), 3/16/1995, pp. 3ff.
122. *Ibid.*, p. 3, n. 4.
123. *Ibid.*, p. 4, n. 7. Although in the beginning of the document Msgr. Hume admits the moral culpability of homosexual genital acts, later on he relativizes by emphasizing the subjective aspect. He states: "Although homosexual genital acts are objectively wrong, nonetheless, the Church warns against generalizations in attributing culpability in individual cases" (*Ibid.*, p. 5, n. 16).

ual, such as mimicking the opposite sex in speaking, dressing, walking and public behavior, taking hormones to assume the characteristics of the opposite sex and even the ever less rare practice of breast implantation or suppressing and surgically altering sex organs. Such practices appear to have been excluded from what the Cardinal considers "genital acts" and are, therefore, indifferent, as he sees it, from the moral standpoint. This is an aberration with regard to morals and Catholic doctrine.

§ 84 *Third:* Cardinal Hume says that "the particular orientation or inclination of the homosexual person is not a moral failing." What does he mean here by "particular orientation or inclination," which others call "tendency"? We have just seen that such a non-immoral inclination cannot consist of sinful consent in the realm of thought, word or deed. Hence, for one to admit a non-condemnable homosexual tendency, one should expect it to be repressed, without any external manifestation and without a right to exist even inside the person's mind. This is all the more certain since the Church has always condemned as a sin the entertainment of thoughts of carnal desire for someone of the opposite sex, even though this relationship is according to nature. Hence homosexual thoughts and desires, being against nature, are all the more sinful, that is to say, morally wrong. This airtight understanding of the homosexual "tendency" is indispensable for one who honestly wishes to teach Catholic thinking. Otherwise, the "tendency" is given such amplitude that the moral vice of homosexuality can almost receive the right to exist, so long as the sexual act is not directly involved.

This, then, is the question to be asked: Who will profit from the imprecision and ambiguity of the Cardinal Primate of England?

§ 85 *Fourth:* Cardinal Hume is gravely mistaken in saying that "the Church does not define or label them [people] in terms of their sexual orientation." For the sin of homosexuality, called the sin against nature, was always considered one of the sins that cry out to Heaven and clamor to God for vengeance. Hence Church teaching and customs place a deservedly infamous note on people who commit such sins.

§ 86 *Fifth:* The Cardinal also says that "the Church recognizes the dignity of all people." Does this sentence, applied to homosexuals, mean that the latter have dignity insofar as they publicly manifest themselves as such, and therefore the Church respects them? Here again one finds imprecision and ambiguity in concepts. Just what is this dignity that the Church recognizes in every person? There are three types of dignity that it would be opportune to distinguish:

§ 87 *Ontological dignity.* All spiritual beings created by God—angels and humans—are created to His image and, as such, are worthy of respect. In this sense, the devil himself, despite his antagonism toward God, continues to maintain his ontological dignity as a spiritual being and thus deserves a certain respect.

§ 88 *Moral dignity.* Superior to ontological dignity is moral dignity, since every being gifted with intellect and will can become similar to God by adhering to good and rejecting evil. Being made to the image of God results in ontological dignity; similarity with God results in moral dignity. In this sense, only men who practice good have dignity, whereas those who practice evil are unworthy.

To this is added yet another characteristic of moral dignity: the internal and external practice of good. So far as the internal practice of good and evil is concerned, a person is judged only by God; so far as the external practice of good and evil goes, the person's acts can be judged by those who see him carry them out. Beyond this, he is judged by the Catholic Church, the custodian of upright morals and good customs. This is why she proposes the example of the Saints, recognizing in them the highest moral dignity that comes from the external, constant and heroic practice of good, and grants them the highest expression of respect by elevating them to the altar. In the opposite sense, the Church censures public and scandalous sinners and calls on her children to avoid them. Obviously, such a censure can brand sinners with a note of shame and, at times, of "*infamy*," which are consequences of their moral unworthiness.

§ 89 *Social dignity.* Social dignity is a concept derived from the collective acceptance by a given society of the ensemble of attitudes that characterizes someone's social profile. In well-established societies, such a concept is based on natural law and natural ethics, whence it derives. According to Church doctrine, a person's social dignity is directly related to his moral dignity. That is, the Church should strive for the social body to be consonant with her morals. This or that concession to principles different from Catholic ones—for example, living in an ambiance of polygamy in certain African countries—can be admitted only as a lesser evil, on a provisional basis, and must cease as soon as possible.

§ 90 Given such clearly defined concepts of the notion of dignity, a question comes to the fore: In what sense could one admit Cardinal Hume's statement that "the Church recognizes the dignity of all people"? As we see it, there is only one meaning wherein the concept is reconcilable with Catholic doctrine in relation to homosexuals: ontological dignity. In respect to moral dignity, homosexuals who publicly declare themselves as such are public, scandalous sinners, whose situation is aggravated even further by the fact that homosexual practice is contrary to nature. To admit self-proclaimed homosexuals as morally indifferent would be to relativize the concepts of good and evil and to subvert the natural order. The same can be said in relation to social dignity.

§ 91 In our view, these point out the main equivocations and illustrate the inexactitude of Cardinal Hume in establishing the premises for his document. One would say that as a whole these equivocations are apt to grant a comfortable moral and social right of citizenship to one of the worst vices ever known.

Incidentally, the English Cardinal's intent to grant moral and social legitimacy to homosexuals reveals itself in other parts of his "Note." Some of the more significant texts include the following:

- "Love between two persons, whether of the same sex or of a different sex, is to be treasured and respected."[124]
- "To love another, whether of the same sex or of a different sex, is to have entered the area of the richest human experience."[125]
- "It is a fundamental human right of every person, irrespective of sexual orientation, to be treated by individuals and by society with dignity, respect, and fairness."[126]
- "Nothing in the Church's teaching can be said to support or sanction, even implicitly, the victimization of homosexual men and women."[127]

---

124. *Ibid.*, p. 4, n. 9.
125. *Ibid.*, p. 4, n. 10.
126. *Ibid.*, p. 4, n. 12.
127. *Ibid.*, p. 5, n. 15. What does the Cardinal understand by "victimization"? In the preceding paragraph he said: "The Church condemns violence of speech or action against homosexual people" (*ibid.*, p. 5, n. 14).

With respect to violent action, the Church certainly condemns taking justice into one's own hands, that is, for a private person to take

- "Furthermore, 'homophobia' should have no place among Catholics."[128]

Such are the advantages that the document of the Cardinal-Archbishop of Westminster procures for homosexuals that one would say his statement is intended as a writ of citizenship for homosexuality in the moral, social and legal domains.

§ 92 From the *political-ecclesiastical* standpoint, it is noteworthy that the Cardinal was pressed to go public with his statement by the homosexual group OutRage. "In January this year," says the London paper *The Daily Mail*, "[Peter] Tatchell sent a letter to the Cardinal which was described as 'forceful.' . . . Cardinal Hume had not intended immediate publication, *Catholic Herald* editor Christina Odone claimed, but did so only when Mr. Tatchell contacted media organizations offering the statement as a 'leaked document.' Tatchell said the statement was a direct response to OutRage's demands, adding: 'When I told them I was going to publish it, they rushed out the state-

---

on the role of judge and executioner against homosexuals. To admit such violence would be tantamount to ignoring legitimately established order and plunging society into chaos. Nonetheless, just as the Church supports equitable punishment for voluntary homicide, oppressing widows and orphans, and denying a defenseless person a just wage, so likewise she can and should support just legal measures punishing acts of sodomy. One can see, therefore, that Cardinal Hume generalizes excessively by failing to consider the possibility of legislation that punishes homosexual acts with punitive action.

As for the other types of violence condemned by the Cardinal, the question once again should be asked: Just what is "violence of speech"? To say that homosexuality is a vice and sodomy a sin that cries out to God for vengeance? To publicly condemn such a sin? To surround it with a note of infamy? Does working to have society and the State discriminate against proven or self-proclaimed homosexuals amount to "victimizing" or exerting unjust violence against them? If this hypothesis is true, the Cardinal would be condemning Catholic doctrine. If this is a true interpretation of the Cardinal's words, then what Church is he speaking of when he states that the Church does not sanction violence of speech against homosexuals?

128. *Ibid.*, p. 5, n. 15.

ment themselves.' The Cardinal's office denied that the statement had been issued in a hurry."[129]

As a confirmation that the Cardinal went public out of fear that Peter Tatchell and OutRage might publish even more compromising information, we will present a summary of the facts that took place during those days in Britain to gauge the strength of the homosexuals' threats of blackmail and to see the kind of support Cardinal Hume finds himself receiving.

If we go outside the Catholic arena, we will see that already in November of 1994, OutRage had "outed" (revealed the homosexuality of) ten Anglican bishops.[130] On March 7, the same day that the "Hume document" came to light, the Church of Scotland assembled and issued a statement asking for more tolerance and understanding for homosexuality, in line with the principles upheld by Cardinal Hume.[131]

In view of these facts, Tim Hopkins, director of a group that advocates law reform, called on Cardinal Thomas Winning, head of the Catholic Church in Scotland, to express public support for the interpretations of his English colleague. Through his spokesman, Fr. Tom Connelly, Cardinal Winning said that Cardinal Hume's viewpoints "are entirely in line with the Church's general moral principles."[132]

In a broadcast on BBC television the same night, Scottish bishop Derk Rawcliffe "outed" himself, that is, he openly stated that he "was always a homosexual" and advocated that a blessing be given to relationships among homosexual priests.[133] On March 13, after receiv-

---

129. Anthony Doran—Steve Doughty, "How the gay lobby railroaded a Cardinal," in *The Daily Mail* (London), 3/8/1995; Christina Frade, "*El sexo de los Obispos*," in *El Mundo* (Madrid), 3/19/1995, p. 2.
130. Greg Hadfield, "This Is Just a Start, Say the Activists, in *The Daily Mail*, 3/18/1995; Ruth Gledhill, "Churchmen condemn move to 'Out' Hope," in *The Times*, 3/15/1995; Luca Romano, "Estremisti omosex minacciano di fari I nomi di prelati e deputati," in *Il Giornale*, 3/15/1995.
131. Ray Clancy, "Church Pleads for Greater Tolerance of Homosexuals," in *The Daily Telegraph*, 3/8/1995.
132. Severin Carrel, "Cardinal Winning Challenged to Back Praise for Gay Love," in *The Scotsman*, 3/8/1995.
133. *Ibid.*; "Bispo anglicano admite que é homossexual," *O Globo*, 3/9/1995; G. Hadfield, *ibid.*; Murray White, "Cardinal Launches

ing a letter from the leader of OutRage, the Anglican bishop of London, David Hope, published a letter saying he was neither heterosexual nor homosexual, since his sexuality resided in an ambiguous "gray area."[134] He also promised tolerance toward homosexuals. Hope condemned OutRage's campaign as "profoundly disturbing, based almost totally on rumors and unknown sources, and intimidating in nature."[135] Some people viewed his words as a semi-confession.[136]

On March 14, Hope's statement received a letter of support from 34 primates of the Anglican church assembled in Windsor. The Anglican archbishop of Canterbury, speaking in the name of the other bishops present, manifested to Hope his solidarity, "deploring this reprehensible intrusion into his private life" and manifesting his "most profound affection" and "prayerful support" for the London bishop.[137] On that same day, the Anglican bishop of Southwark, Robert Williamson, said he "would be happy to ordain an openly homosexual priest" living in a stable relationship with someone of the same sex.[138]

Attack on Homophobia," in *The Catholic Herald*, 3/10/1995; *Rogério Simões,* "Bispo anglicano defende sacerdotes homossexuais," in *Folha de S. Paulo*, 4/9/1995.

134. R. Gledhill, *ibid.*; L. Romano, *ibid.*; Allan Massie, "Terror tactics of the Tatchell gang," in *The Daily Telegraph,* 3/15/1995.
135. David Hope, Letter, March 3, 1995, in R. Gledhill, *ibid.*
136. L. Romano, *ibid.*
137. George Carey, Letter of March 14, 1995, in Dan Conagham, "Archbishops Angry at Hope 'Intrusion,'" in *The Daily Telegraph*, 3/15/1995.

    The article by Alessio Alticheri, "Promosso il vescovo gay," in *Corriere della Sera* (4/12/1995) confirms Hope's semi-confession (Note 136) and the prestige the Anglican church sought to give him. According to Alticheri, Hope was given a promotion in the Anglican hierarchy and transferred from the London diocese to that of York, which has above it only the bishop of Canterbury. Hope's promotion was the object of new congratulations and hundreds of letters. "Many came from outside the church, many from homosexuals, some of them really touching," said Hope, second in command of the Anglican church.
138. Robert Williamson, Statement to the press, in R. Gledhill, *ibid.*; A. Massie, *ibid.*

On the 15th of the month, the Anglican archbishop of York, John Habgood, published in *The Times* an article stating: "The common presumption that all physical intimacy must lead to penetrative sex is unjust to those who want to enjoy some warmth of companionship, but wish to draw a line."[139]

The 34 Anglican bishops who were gathered in an international conference issued a document that said: "In the internal life of the church, there are models of sexuality different from those recalled by traditional Christian morals; nevertheless, these experiences are marked by a genuine Christian seal."[140] In that regard, the *Corriere della Sera* comments: "A success, organizations for the defense of gay rights rejoiced. . . . the Anglican church admits one can simultaneously be gay and a good Christian."[141]

Following Cardinal Hume's orientation, the group Catholic Aids Link published a 38-page booklet entitled *Positively Called*, in which it claims that "many HIV-infected clergy and religious are able not only to maintain their active ministry but . . . are uniquely suited to play a special role in the Church's pastoral ministry in the HIV/AIDS epidemic."[142] "It is certainly plausible that God could call to religious or priestly life some infected with HIV," adds the report, which has the backing of the English hierarchy.[143]

The journalist of *The Catholic Herald* adds: "*Positively Called*, which was culled from seminars held for those selecting candidates for the priesthood, urges the Church to act in an 'inclusive' way towards those 'who may have acquired HIV through activity not permissible under vows,' rather than treating them as 'paedophiles.' "[144] The publication, the journalist concludes, results "at least indirectly, from intense lobbying by the militant homosexual group OutRage." "Peter Tatchell," the reporter continues, "claims to have written to

---

139. John Habgood, "When Sex Ceases to Be Private," in *The Times*, 3/15/1995.
140. 34 Anglican Bishops, Statements, in "I gay? Bravi cristiani," in *Corriere della Sera*, 3/17/1995.
141. *Corriere della Sera, ibid.*
142. Catholic Aids Link, *Positively Called*, in Piers McGrandle, "Church Needs HIV Clergy Says Group," in *The Catholic Herald*, 3/17/1995.
143. *Ibid.*
144. P. McGrandle, *ibid.*

four senior Catholic clergy and two more Anglican clergy urging them to 'come out.' "[145]

Another commentator reported that Tatchell was preparing to "out" another five Anglican bishops.[146] The *Corriere della Sera* reported these arrogant words spoken by the homosexual leader: "We will influence the future policy of the Church of England in a way that no one can imagine."[147,148]

After his latest threats, Tatchell opened a new front of attack by sending letters to twenty members of Parliament—two of them ministers in John Major's cabinet—suggesting that they publicly admit their homosexuality. The letters exhorted recipients to "follow the example of the two MP's who admitted their homosexuality."[149]

Cardinal Hume's statement on homosexuality can be objectively situated within the context of this great blackmailing plot being carried out by homosexual groups against Catholic prelates, Anglican bishops, the Church of Scotland and English cabinet ministers and members of Parliament. As a whole, the Cardinal's document is by far, in our view, the strategic piece of greatest importance and usefulness for homosexual interests in England.

§ 93 In **Italy**, an unusual survey was carried out by German reporter Edwin Thomas of *Micromega* magazine. Every evening for several weeks, Thomas would stroll in the environs of St. Peter's Basilica. In that period, he claims to have been approached by 64 churchmen who made homosexual propositions to him. Thomas says they were ecclesiastics "of all kinds, from seminarians to the secretary of a nunciature."[150]

§ 94 We cannot omit the events that occurred at the Vatican at the end of 1989 during an International Conference on AIDS promoted by

---

145. *Ibid.*
146. Peter Tatchell, Statement, in Mino Vignolo, "Preti e politici gay dovete confessare," in *Corriere della Sera*, 3/21/1995.
147. L. Romano, *ibid.*
148. P. Tatchell, Statement, *ibid.*
149. *O Globo*, "Grupo gay inglês ameaça revelar lista de políticos homossexuais," 3/21/1995; L. Romano, *ibid.*; M. Vignolo, *ibid.*
150. Edwin Thomas, "Amori gay all'ombra del cupulone. Inchiesta di *Micromega* fra sacerdoti omosessuali," in *Adista*, 5/13/1995, pp. 8f.

the Holy See. The three-day event brought together 1,400 Bishops, theologians, scientists and researchers from 85 countries.

Right in the opening session, Irish priest John White stood up in Synod Hall and displayed a sign reading: "The Church has AIDS." As he was ushered out, White announced, "I have AIDS and live with it every day."[151]

Later, AIDS sufferer Peter Larking of London engaged in a heated exchange with conference organizer, Archbishop Fiorenzo Angelini, and finally stormed out.

The following day, however, Archbishop Angelini readmitted Fr. White to the conference with a public embrace.[152] AIDS victim Larking was also allowed to return and was even granted a brief audience with John Paul II, who told him, "I'm praying for you."[153]

CONCLUSION

§ 95 Nothing appeared more fitting for us to close this overall view of homosexuality than an excerpt from the *Liber Gomorrhianus* (*Book of Gomorrha*) of Saint Peter Damian (1007-1072). The work was offered to Saint Leo IX (1002-1054), who was Pope during the years 1049-1054,[154] as a tool to help reform customs in the clergy, a pressing issue at the time. This movement was known as the Gregorian Reform, since to a large extent it was inspired by the monk Hildebrand, later Pope Saint Gregory VII.

Saint Leo IX glowingly praised Saint Peter Damian's book:[155]

---

151. "Aids é debatida no Vaticano," *O Estado de S. Paulo*, 11/14/1989.
152. Rod Norland, "'The Church Has AIDS'—Anger Flares at a Vatican Conference," in *Newsweek*, 11/27/1989, p. 55.
153. *Ibid.*
154. Those wishing to know more on the death of Saint Leo IX as a result of the wars he personally led against the Normans who invaded papal territories are referred to Emile Amann, *Papes imperiaux et Papes romains,* in V.A., *Histoire de l'Eglise*, vol. VII, pp. 105ff.
155. While Leo IX praised Saint Peter Damian's book, the same Pope later censured a certain harshness in the work. Leo noted that not all who engage in homosexual acts are equally sinful and thus not all merit

"Leo, Bishop, servant of the servants of God, to the beloved son in Christ, Peter the hermit, the joy of eternal blessing.

"The book, beloved son, which with noble style and even more noble intention you have published . . . shows with clear documents that by applying your intelligence you have attained, through pious effort, the apex of a refined purity. For you, who thus raised the arm of the spirit against the obscenity of lust, have overcome the disorder of the flesh, an execrable vice that removes people far from the Author of virtues, who, being pure, admits nothing impure. And His inheritance will not belong to those who indulge in sordid pleasures. . . .

"Most dear son, I rejoice in untold manner that you preach, by the example of your behavior, all that you have taught through the gift of oratory. Indeed, it is more holy to preach through works than words. For this reason, by doing God's work, you will obtain the palm of victory and, with God [the Father] and with the Virgin's Son, you will rejoice in the eternal mansion filled with as many rewards as the people you wrenched from the snares of the demon, and these people will serve as your retinue and, in a certain way, will crown you."[156]

These are Saint Peter Damian's words lambasting the vice of sodomy:

"In fact, this vice is absolutely not comparable to any others, because its enormity supersedes them all. Indeed, this vice produces the death of bodies and the destruction of souls. It pollutes the flesh, extinguishes the light of reason, expels the Holy Ghost from His temple in man's heart and introduces into it the devil who is the instigator of lust; it leads into error, totally expels truth from the deceived soul, sets up traps for those who fall into it, then caps the well to prevent those who fall into it from getting out, opens the gates of Hell and closes the door of Heaven to them, turns a former citizen of the heavenly Jerusalem into an heir of the infernal Babylon, transforming him from a heavenly star into a straw for the eternal fire, wrenches

---

the same ecclesiastical censure. He also said that it is not always necessary to depose a cleric for this reason. *Mansi* XIX, cols. 685-686, in McNeill, *op. cit.*, pp. 80-81.

156. St. Leo IX, *Epistula super Librum gomorrhianum,* in PL 145, cols. 159f.

a member away from the Church and plunges him into the voracious flames of the fiery Gehenna.

"This vice strives to destroy the walls of one's heavenly motherland and rebuild those of devastated Sodom. Indeed, it violates temperance, kills purity, stifles chastity and annihilates virginity—which is irrecoverable—with the sword of a most infamous union. It infects everything, stains everything, pollutes everything; it leaves nothing pure, nothing but filth. 'All things are clean to the clean,' as the Apostle says, 'but to them that are defiled, and to unbelievers, nothing is clean; but both their mind and their conscience are defiled' (*Titus* 1:15).

"This vice expels one from the choir of the ecclesiastical host and obliges one to join the possessed and those who work in league with the devil; it separates the soul from God and links it with demons. This most pestiferous queen of the Sodomites makes those who obey her tyrannical laws repugnant to men and hateful to God; it [this sin] wages a nefarious war against God and obliges the person to enlist in the ranks of the perverse spirit; it separates him from the company of Angels and deprives his soul of its nobility; it imposes on the unfortunate soul the yoke of its own domination. It tears its henchmen from the arms of virtue and exposes them as prey to the arrows of all vices. It humiliates at church, condemns at court, defiles in secret, dishonors in public, gnaws at the person's conscience like a worm and burns his flesh like fire. . . .

"Miserable flesh burns with the fire of lust, cold intelligence trembles under the rancor of suspicion, and the unfortunate man's heart is possessed by hellish chaos, subjecting him to as many pains of conscience as he is tortured in punishment. Yes, as soon as the most venomous serpent plunges its fangs into the unfortunate soul, it is immediately deprived of its senses and memory; the edge of his intelligence is dulled, he forgets God and even himself.

"Indeed, this scourge destroys the foundations of the faith, weakens the forces of hope, dissipates the bonds of charity, annihilates justice, undermines fortitude, eliminates hope and dulls the edge of prudence.

"And what else shall I say? It expels all the forces of virtue from the temple of the human heart and, pulling the door from its hinges, introduces into it all the barbarity of vice . . .

"In effect, the one whom . . . this most atrocious beast has swallowed down its bloody throat is prevented, by the weight of his chains, from practicing all good works and is precipitated into all the abysses of its uttermost wickedness. Thus, as soon as someone has fallen into this abyss of extreme perdition, he is exiled from the heavenly motherland, separated from the Body of Christ, confounded by the authority of the whole Church, condemned by the judgment of all the Holy Fathers, despised by men on earth and reproved by the society of heavenly citizens; he creates for himself an earth of iron and a sky of bronze. On the one hand, laden with the weight of his crime, he is unable to rise; on the other hand, he is no longer able to conceal his evil in the refuge of ignorance. He cannot be happy while he lives nor have hope when he dies, because now he is obliged to suffer the ignominy of men's derision and later, the torment of eternal condemnation."[157, *]

157. St. Peter Damian, *op. cit.*, cols. 175ff.

* *Publisher's Note*: Lest anyone receive the impression from St. Peter Damian's words that repentance is impossible after sins of sodomy, we draw the Reader's attention to the words of Pope St. Leo IX (p. 61 above) regarding the people whom St. Peter Damian will wrench from the snares of the demon and who will serve as his retinue in Heaven. Repentance from any sin is possible, but St. Peter Damian seems to be saying that sins of homosexuality are the most difficult sins from which to repent.

Scripture Alone? 21 Reasons to Reject *Sola Scriptura. Peters* 2.00
Spiritual Exercises. *St. Ignatius Loyola* 12.50
St. Gerard Majella. *Fr. Saint-Omer, C.SS.R.* 8.50
Mystical City of God—Abridged. *Ven. Mary of Agreda* 18.50
Moments Divine—Before the Blessed Sacrament. *Reuter* 8.50
Miraculous Images of Our Lady. *Cruz* 20.00
Miraculous Images of Our Lord. *Cruz* 13.50
Raised from the Dead. *Fr. Hebert* 16.50
Love and Service of God, Infinite Love. *Mother Louise Margaret* 12.50
Life and Work of Mother Louise Margaret. *Fr. O'Connell* 12.50
Autobiography of St. Margaret Mary. 5.00
Thoughts and Sayings of St. Margaret Mary 5.00
The Voice of the Saints. *Comp. by Francis Johnston* 6.00
The 12 Steps to Holiness and Salvation. *St. Alphonsus* 7.50
The Rosary and the Crisis of Faith. *Cirrincione & Nelson* 2.00
Sin and Its Consequences. *Cardinal Manning* 7.00
Fourfold Sovereignty of God. *Cardinal Manning* 5.00
Dialogue of St. Catherine of Siena. *Transl. Algar Thorold* 10.00
Catholic Answer to Jehovah's Witnesses. *D'Angelo* 10.00
Twelve Promises of the Sacred Heart. (100 cards) 5.00
Life of St. Aloysius Gonzaga. *Fr. Meschler* 12.00
The Love of Mary. *D. Roberto* 8.00
Begone Satan. *Fr. Vogl* 3.00
The Prophets and Our Times. *Fr. R. G. Culleton* 13.50
St. Therese, The Little Flower. *John Beevers* 6.00
St. Joseph of Copertino. *Fr. Angelo Pastrovicchi* 6.00
Mary, The Second Eve. *Cardinal Newman* 2.50
Devotion to Infant Jesus of Prague. *Booklet* 75
Reign of Christ the King in Public & Private Life. *Davies* 1.25
The Wonder of Guadalupe. *Francis Johnston* 7.50
Apologetics. *Msgr. Paul Glenn* 10.00
Baltimore Catechism No. 1 . . . . 3.50
Baltimore Catechism No. 2 . . . . 4.50
Baltimore Catechism No. 3 . . . . 8.00
An Explanation of the Baltimore Catechism. *Fr. Kinkead* 16.50
Bethlehem. *Fr. Faber* 18.00
Bible History. *Schuster* 10.00
Blessed Eucharist. *Fr. Mueller* 9.00
Catholic Catechism. *Fr. Faerber* 7.00
The Devil. *Fr. Delaporte* 6.00
Dogmatic Theology for the Laity. *Fr. Premm* 20.00
Evidence of Satan in the Modern World. *Cristiani* 10.00
Fifteen Promises of Mary. (100 cards) 5.00
Life of Anne Catherine Emmerich. 2 vols. *Schmoeger* 37.50
Life of the Blessed Virgin Mary. *Emmerich* 16.50
Manual of Practical Devotion to St. Joseph. *Patrignani* 15.00
Prayer to St. Michael. (100 leaflets) 5.00
Prayerbook of Favorite Litanies. *Fr. Hebert* 10.00
Preparation for Death. (Abridged). *St. Alphonsus* 8.00
Purgatory Explained. *Schouppe* 13.50
Purgatory Explained. (pocket, unabr.). *Schouppe* 9.00
Fundamentals of Catholic Dogma. *Ludwig Ott* 21.00
Spiritual Conferences. *Tauler* 13.00
Trustful Surrender to Divine Providence. *Bl. Claude* 5.00
Wife, Mother and Mystic. *Bessieres* 8.00

Prices subject to change.

St. Teresa of Avila. *Forbes* 6.00
St. Ignatius Loyola. *Forbes* 6.00
St. Catherine of Siena. *Forbes* 6.00
The Agony of Jesus. *Padre Pio* 1.50
Sermons of the Curé of Ars. *Vianney* 12.50
St. Antony of the Desert. *St. Athanasius* 5.00
Is It a Saint's Name? *Fr. William Dunne* 2.50
St. Pius V—His Life, Times, Miracles. *Anderson* 4.50
Who Is Therese Neumann? *Fr. Charles Carty.* 2.00
Martyrs of the Coliseum. *Fr. O'Reilly.* 18.50
Way of the Cross. *St. Alphonsus Liguori* 1.00
Way of the Cross. *Franciscan version* 1.00
How Christ Said the First Mass. *Fr. Meagher* 18.50
Too Busy for God? Think Again! *D'Angelo* 5.00
St. Bernadette Soubirous. *Trochu* 18.50
Passion and Death of Jesus Christ. *Liguori* 10.00
Treatise on the Love of God. 1 Vol. *St. Francis de Sales* 24.00
Confession Quizzes. *Radio Replies Press* 1.50
St. Philip Neri. *Fr. V. J. Matthews.* 5.50
St. Louise de Marillac. *Sr. Vincent Regnault* 6.00
The Old World and America. *Rev. Philip Furlong* 18.00
Prophecy for Today. *Edward Connor* 5.50
The Book of Infinite Love. *Mother de la Touche* 5.00
Chats with Converts. *Fr. M. D. Forrest.* 10.00
The Church Teaches. *Church Documents* 16.50
Conversation with Christ. *Peter T. Rohrbach* 10.00
Purgatory and Heaven. *J. P. Arendzen* 5.00
Liberalism Is a Sin. *Sarda y Salvany* 7.50
Spiritual Legacy of Sr. Mary of the Trinity. *van den Broek* 10.00
The Creator and the Creature. *Fr. Frederick Faber* 16.50
Radio Replies. *3* Vols. *Frs. Rumble and Carty* 42.00
Convert's Catechism of Catholic Doctrine. *Fr. Geiermann* 3.00
Incarnation, Birth, Infancy of Jesus Christ. *St. Alphonsus* 10.00
Light and Peace. *Fr. R. P. Quadrupani* 7.00
Dogmatic Canons & Decrees of Trent, Vat. I. *Documents* 9.50
The Evolution Hoax Exposed. *A. N. Field* 6.00
The Primitive Church. *Fr. D. I. Lanslots.* 10.00
The Priest, the Man of God. *St. Joseph Cafasso* 13.50
Blessed Sacrament. *Fr. Frederick Faber* 18.50
Christ Denied. *Fr. Paul Wickens* 2.50
New Regulations on Indulgences. *Fr. Winfrid Herbst* 2.50
A Tour of the Summa. *Msgr. Paul Glenn* 18.00
Spiritual Conferences. *Fr. Frederick Faber* 15.00
Latin Grammar. *Scanlon and Scanlon* 16.50
A Brief Life of Christ. *Fr. Rumble* 2.00
Marriage Quizzes. *Radio Replies Press* 1.50
True Church Quizzes. *Radio Replies Press* 1.50
The Secret of the Rosary. *St. Louis De Montfort* 3.00
Mary, Mother of the Church. *Church Documents* 4.00
The Sacred Heart and the Priesthood. *de la Touche* 9.00
Revelations of St. Bridget. *St. Bridget of Sweden* 3.00
Magnificent Prayers. *St. Bridget of Sweden* 2.00
The Happiness of Heaven. *Fr. J. Boudreau* 8.00
St. Catherine Labouré of the Miraculous Medal. *Dirvin* 13.50
The Glories of Mary. (pocket, unabr.). *St. Alphonsus Liguori* 10.00

Prices subject to change.